THE **JOB SEARCH** HANDBOOK

THE JOB SEARCH HANDBOOK

by
JOHN NOBLE

**Associate Director
of Career Services,
Harvard University**

BOB ADAMS, INC. ● BOSTON

Published by
Bob Adams, Inc.
840 Summer Street
Boston MA   02127

Cover design by Giselle deGuzman.

ISBN 0-937860-90-5

Also from Bob Adams, Inc.:

> *The Job Bank Series (area-specific guides to employment in major American cities)*
>
> *Knock 'em Dead With Great Answers to Tough Interview Questions, by Martin John Yate.*
>
> *Careers and the College Grad, edited by Gigi Ranno.*
>
> *Career Paths, edited by Michael Fiedler*
>
> *Job Search Strategy for College Grads, by Susan Bernard and Gretchen Thompson.*

To order the above books, or additional copies of this book, call 1-800-USA-JOBS.

To Abigail.

CONTENTS

CHAPTER FOUR:
Negotiations, Careers, and Job Satisfaction   103

Managing Your Success/ Evaluating Offers/ Negotiation/ Some Dilemmas In "Winding It All Up"/ Ending The Job Hunt In Style/ Planning Your Future and Career/ Changing Your Career Goals/ Dealing With Setbacks/ The Team Player -- and the "We" Generation

APPENDIX:
Assessing Your Skills, Identifying Goals, and Doing the Research   121

Pre-Search Researching/ Know What You Want/ Assess Yourself/ Finding the "Perfect" Job/ The Paper Chase: Where to Get Information/ The Psychology of the Want Ad -- and the Personnel Office/ Sample Job Search Notebook Worksheet

ACKNOWLEDGMENTS

Well-deserved thanks go to the staff at Harvard's Office of Career Services, who have helped to provide a super support group for my counseling and writing, especially Ann Martin and Marty Leape.

PREFACE

One of the first job interviews I ever had was with the programming director of a Boston television station. I was interested in exploring a career in educational television, and had the good fortune to get a courtesy meeting with the local affiliate's top man. I thought I knew a great deal about the field. After all, hadn't I spent the fifties and sixties glued to the set just like any other baby boomer? Surely I could do the job, whatever it was.

I walked into that meeting confident that some positive lead, if not a job, would present itself. It didn't. Twenty minutes later, walking back to my car, I realized that I had probably just blown an ideal opportunity.

As though to underscore the errors of my ways, the job hunting gods decided to lock me out of my car. For better or for worse, I had some time to reflect on the meeting I'd just left. As I stood there, coat hanger in hand, I came to the brilliant conclusion that I had been woefully unprepared for the meeting.

This sad tale is intended to point out the importance of preparation -- and of perspective. Preparation is only effective if you bear in mind the point of view held by the *person for whom you're preparing.* I thought I was prepared for that meeting. The programming director thought he was wasting his time. Whose perspective had I been more concerned about beforehand?

Successful job hunting depends upon how well you appreciate the interviewer's point of view. Every aspect of job hunting, from your resume to your acceptance of a job offer, must reflect a knowledge of the problems and challenges that face the employer.

The aim of this book is to provide you with the basic information needed to get your job hunt off the ground quickly. There is nothing more frustrating than wishing you could make a career move -- but lacking the information necessary to move forward. In the pages that follow, I've tried not only to pass along that information, but also to bring a light touch to a very serious job -- finding one.

John Noble

Cambridge, Massachusetts

CHAPTER ONE:
Getting Your Foot
In The Door

GETTING STARTED

It's time to get a job.

Whether you're changing positions, re-entering the job market after a long absence, trying to put your college degree to work, or conducting your first full-fledged job search, you should be familiar with certain basic principles that are essential to finding professional employment. This book will introduce you to those principles quickly and concisely.

The most important of those principles is a simple one. It underlies everything else you'll do during your job search. That principle is to think like an employer.

This book will start with the basics on virtually every aspect of the job hunt; however, one of the working assumptions is that you already know the answers to a few very important questions. These "fundamental" queries include: What you want to do? What industry you want to do it in? What are some pertinent facts about the companies that you wish to target for your future employment?

If you feel that you need some extra ideas in tackling these matters, take some time to look over the Appendix at the end of the book before beginning your job search in earnest. This section provides you with an easy-to-follow program that will allow you to conduct a complete research campaign. It also offers some important tips on identifying your professional strengths and weaknesses.

For now, the concern is with the fundamentals of executing a winning job search. That means that topic number one is "people."

PEOPLE: MAKING CONTACT

People are perhaps the most important source of information about new jobs -- or, for that matter, whole new careers. This may seem obvious, but it's a point that many fail to catch. There's still a great deal of truth to the familiar phrase, "It's not what you know, it's who you know that really counts." Today, though, the more accurate summation might begin, "It's not *only* what you know..."

Make no mistake. No matter who your contacts are, you will never stay in a job for which you do not have the skills. But the fact remains that the most successful way to get a new job is with the help of other people. Ultimately, you'll have to rely on people -- even if it's only the person making the final hiring decision!

In practice, you'll incorporate a great many more people into your efforts than the one person hiring you. In fact, the more people you involve, the better. It is essential for you to develop a network of people within an industry with whom you're on familiar terms.

You'll be approaching these people for information. You won't be asking for a job... yet. You're after hard facts right now. These facts will be invaluable to you when you pursue the employers you've targeted.

At this point you may be saying to yourself, "I don't know anybody! I'm doomed!" Don't panic. Nobody begins life with a full complement of professional associates. Everyone starts somewhere. As a matter of fact, "starting fresh" may work to your advantage in some instances.

Consider the case of the job hunter who asked a friend to "put in a word for him" to the search committee pondering his application. A number of words got put in -- with the best of intentions -- but these included some awkward facts the job hunter would have rather detoured around. The "contact" chattered away about how her friend was looking for something that would leave him plenty of free time to pursue other activities on the side, and that he felt he'd been badly overworked at his previous job. Neither revelation scored points with the committee. His application was shelved.

You don't just want a contact network. You want an effective contact network. One that you can use to glean information, make positive impressions, and keep future career avenues open. So: where to begin?

Suppose you're interested in a position as a guidance

counselor at a small area college. Your academic background provides a good match, and you feel perfect for the job, but you don't know anyone at the college. What should you do?

Go to the guidance center. Ask the people in the reception area for some information about the services provided -- pamphlets, brochures, bulletins, or newsletters are probably on display there. If anyone asks why you are interested in these materials, be honest. Say that you are applying for a job and that you want to get some information about the center, its staff, and its facilities so that you can make an informed application. Be pleasant. Act professionally. Ask politely for the name of the person to whom you're speaking. Later, you'll probably want to jot this name down for future reference -- for instance, as the contact in a cover letter. It's a good idea to keep up a "job search notebook": a repository for all the pertinent information you come across. (See the Appendix for a sample page from such a notebook.)

Chances are that the person helping you will ask for your name as well. You may want to take the opportunity to inquire about who is responsible for hiring decisions if this seems appropriate.

With any luck, you now have one or two names, a number of pertinent materials about the center, and perhaps even a vague idea of what the job outlook is like. Not bad at all.

Going straight to the source, then, can be an effective for you to begin building a contact network. But it's not the only way.

Your local newspaper will feature a classified help-wanted section; the listings in it are good sources for leads and potential contacts. A complete discussion of how to use the classified section as a reference can be found in the Appendix; however, it should be noted here that classified ads can provide names that will add measurably to your contact pool. About 75% of all ads will contain the name of a contact person. Though this individual is very likely part of the personnel department (and therefore highly unlikely to make a final hiring decision), make a record of the name if the company or position appeals to you.   It can be useful to have an up-to-date name to use in your future discussions at a given firm.

You may even find a position by following up leads in the classifieds, but don't bet on it: companies that place want ads are usually swamped with applicants, and it's almost impossible to stand out from the pack.   The procedure for pursuing the specific positions you uncover during your research is outlined later in this chapter, in the discussion on the Direct Contact Letter.

The local newspaper provides you with a wide variety of articles and personality profiles, as well.   These are also sources you can use to develop contacts.   Of greatest interest to you is the business section, which you should read regularly.   Bring the perspective of a stockholder or industry executive to the articles you read: look for (and make a note of) the names of the experts, analysts, and company leaders who are quoted.   Believe it or not, you can generate contacts from these names.   You may never reach the president of IBM or the national sales manager of Xerox, but the vast majority of the sources quoted are accessible, and can be contacted by any ordinary human being willing to invest in the time and expense of a phone call.

Suppose, for example, you're interested in retailing. You've just read an article about a new mall opening in a nearby community; quoted prominently are several "spokes-persons" for the major retailers planning to set up operations at the location slated for development.   Each source identified by name in the article as a company representative should become part of your contact list.

When the time comes to speak with these people, you'll probably find favorable responses coming your way. Almost anyone will be flattered to receive a call from someone making reference to (and thereby reinforcing) his or her status as a "newsmaker."   The chances are excellent that you'll be able to arrange some kind of interview or even get a referral.

Resources beyond your local newspaper, of course, should also be explored.   The industry you've chosen probably has some sort of trade journal or magazine that's read by virtually everyone within the field. In show business, this publication would be *Variety;* in publishing, *Publishers Weekly;* one of the specialized livestock magazines is called, daringly enough, *Sheep!* Find out the name of the journal that applies to the field you've selected. Then track down a copy. Beware: subscriptions tend to be expensive. It's a good bet you can find back issues in any large urban library.

A regular feature of most such magazines is its calendar section, describing events and functions of interest to people in the industry. Many of these meetings are open to the public. Take the time and effort to attend one of these functions if at all possible. You will not only find out more about the industry, but you'll also have the opportunity to meet people. So jump right in and make the most of that opportunity. Make a point of meeting as many people as you can. Ask politely for their names. Find out what firms they represent. See how many will tell you how they got started in the business (more than you think will be flattered at the request). The people you speak with, of course, will serve as an initial point of reference at some later point in your job search.

Again, be honest about your interest in their business. Remember that doing so will only be to your advantage. After all, how many job hunters take the initiative to explore careers so thoroughly?

Trade shows and conventions can be fertile job hunting territory. The representatives manning the exhibits are there to talk to the people wandering from booth to booth. Professionals you speak with may not be prepared to talk about specific career opportunities, but they will most likely take the time to give you information about their company. Toward the end of the day, the exhibitors are often so tired from a full day of "working the crowd" that you may actually provide a pleasant break from the grind!

Career fairs are another good contact medium. Employers go to career fairs for two reasons: either to find new prospective employees or to present a positive image of their company as a matter of public relations. Even if the firm is looking for applicants, however, the personnel department will often serve as intermediary -- and will do their best to screen candidates.

Because there may be as much door-closing as door-opening at these affairs, you shouldn't convince yourself that a career fair can mean an on-the-spot job offer. But career fairs can be excellent opportunities to gather valuable, current information about a variety of employment possibilities.

Other contact sources might include your high school and college alumni groups. The old alums are often willing to perpetuate the "old boy network" (in which, thankfully, both "boys" and "girls" seem to be welcome these days). Call your school's alumni office -- there may already be some kind of referral network set up. Some colleges have established career advisory services along these lines. If yours hasn't, all colleges (and many high schools) have some kind of alumni directory. Use it. Concentrate not only on people who've been out of school for some years, but also on more recent grads. Sometimes people in your own class have the best, most practical information as a result of just having gone through the process of finding a job.

Even if you don't know the person you're calling, the two of you do have something in common; that alone is usually a valid reason to initiate the contact. Ask yourself: who would you rather help out, a person from your own college or high school, or someone with you've never heard of in your life? Don't be shy. Explore every possible lead.

BREAKING THE ICE

The fact is, though, most of us are shy to some degree, and meeting new people is never easy. Precisely because this is true, you must develop a system that not only makes you feel comfortable, but also gets you the desired results.

Perhaps meeting people will never feel completely natural. That's okay. But being able to strike up a conversation on a professional level is absolutely necessary if you intend to find a good job. You must take the first step. Believe it or not, most people will respond favorably -- because they, too, are worried about meeting people. By taking the initiative, you've made life easier for them!

Once you've determined where and how you want to meet people -- what exactly do you say?

One excellent way to initiate a conversation with a contact is to ask about his or her job duties or career path. At a convention or meeting, this type of question can provide you with some interesting background information -- and it's a great way to break the ice.

In a letter or phone call, ask the person's advice about an issue of your choice. Most everyone will take the time to give you their perspective. After all, isn't being sought out for counsel a sign of competence in one's field? Your challenge is to turn the advice into an opportunity to speak with the contact again, or to obtain a referral.

Finally, if you feel uncomfortable with either of the above approaches, then display your knowledge of the industry. Make a remark about a recent development or advancement (say, a particularly productive new breed of Dorset you read about in the latest issue of *Sheep!*), and then follow by asking your contact what he or she thinks the implications will be. This, too, will get a conversation moving, display you in a positive light, and more than likely leave you on a first-name basis with the contact.

It's worth repeating: people are the most important link in the job search process. Want ads, job listings, career fairs, mailings -- all can provide some exposure to the job market. But you will find that most opportunities arise once you have begun talking to the people who earn their own living in your chosen field.

Select one or more of the contact options outlined here; then go out and fill up your notebook. Try to identify the person in charge of professional hiring, but do so discreetly. Make a note of the full name, title, and company of each person who helps you. Be sure to enter, as well, any new information about the industry that you can use in your search. Once you've done that, you'll be ready for the next level of contact.

TIME MANAGEMENT:
ON THE JOB WHILE
LOOKING FOR ONE

Thus far it may seem as though an assumption has been made about your schedule: that you have plenty of time to go around chatting with your contacts, peruse newspapers and magazines at your leisure, and attend every trade show or convention in the Western Hemisphere. Obviously, you don't.

In order to carry out an effective job search, you must be extremely well-organized, especially if you're spending 35-40 hours (or more) each week at your current job. You must accept a simple fact: your free time must be put to good use if your job hunt is to end successfully.

Some pessimists might tell you that, if you are holding down a full time job, you don't have the time necessary to carry out a job search, and that anyone who wants to have a real chance at finding something worthwhile should quit his or her present job and devote all available time to the search. Whatever you do, don't be a pessimist -- and don't quit your job.

There are a great many reasons not to quit your job, but as far as your job search is concerned, one time-tested reason towers above the rest. Employers don't trust the unemployed.

It's easy to understand why employers feel this way. There are simply too many variables in the equation once an employer determines that you don't just want a job, you need one. Even if you fit the job description perfectly, it will be difficult to convince the employer to give you a chance. This attitude may be unfair, but it's quite common.

Look at it from the employer's point of view. If you could choose from many candidates with identical, outstanding qualifications, would you choose someone currently on the unemployment line over someone with a steady job? Rightly or wrongly, unemployment indicates instability, disorganization, lack of motivation, and insecurity.

So keep your job! If for some reason you're identified as a victim of an upcoming company layoff, or are certain you're about to be fired, then think about quitting. (In the latter instance, it will probably look better on your resume.) Other than that, stick with it. Even if you are forced into some kind of involuntary exit from a full-time job, think seriously about temporary employment if you don't find a new position within a month or so. You cannot afford to have large time gaps in your employment history.

How do you manage your time while on the job? First, outline how you presently spend your time. If you work from nine to five, how do you spend your mornings, midday breaks, and after work hours? When are you free during the day to pursue other activities?

Think creatively about all the time available to you during the day, as well as your personal and vacation days. Save those precious "excused absence" days for the really important meetings, and try to find time during your regular work day to make phone calls and meet with contacts.

Making the calls that accompany your job search may be a problem if you work for an organization that discourages personal calls. If this is the case, try to find a convenient, discreetly located phone booth that won't be exposed to a lot of background noise. Get a phone credit card so you won't be reduced to carrying your piggy bank in your briefcase, and jingling suspiciously whenever you enter or leave the office.

The best times to call your contacts are just before business hours and during lunch breaks. If your contacts are highly-placed members of the company you're calling, there's a good chance they'll be in to work before nine. Many large companies will operate their switchboards before the standard business day begins at 9 a.m. for the sole purpose of accommodating the early-rising executives.

Calling at the end of the day is also an option, but you may find that your contact is just running out the door, and is neither capable nor eager to talk about job opportunities with you.

The same strategy should apply to setting up meetings.

Many people will be available before 9 a.m., during lunch, or (less frequently) at the end of the day. Buying your contact breakfast or lunch is one memorable way to say "thank you" for the time expended in meeting with you. There's no need to run up a tab at a fancy restauarant. A hot dog in the park for lunch, or a cup of coffee and a "gourmet" danish at your favorite little cafe for breakfast -- each can provide a positive ambience for your meeting.

Evenings are the perfect time to do your research. Spend an hour or so every evening reading and researching your field. The sooner you get into the habit of digesting all the news in your industry on a regular basis, the sooner you'll be able to make important insights into how that industry works. That, of course, is very impressive to contacts.

So be creative -- and realistic -- in your time management. You'll probably find that you have much more time to pursue your job search than you imagined. And because you'll be presenting yourself as a productive, happily employed candidate, you will actually get further than you will if you quit your current job to facilitate contacting people during the day. It bears repeating: do not quit your job unless it is absolutely necessary.

LETTER WRITING

A well-written cover letter (usually included with a resume) can make a significant difference in your success in arranging meetings with potential employers. Fortunately, most job hunters spend little time on their letters; your presentation, therefore, will stand out, because it will look much better!

There is a certain knack to writing a good cover letter. You can develop that knack with a little practice. The key here is to approach the letter as though you were reading it as an employer.

You may ask at this point, "What about the resume?! Shouldn't we be talking about that first?" In a word, no.

Most people consider the resume the most important written element of their job search. They're wrong. Most employers read resumes to screen out prospective candidatcs. In other words, they try to find things they don't like about your background so they can put your application in the "circular file" and reduce the huge pile of job inquiries on their desks. With a cover letter, on the other hand, an employer is usually trying to answer a couple of questions quickly. Who is this person? What can they offer me? What do they want?

That's the mindset you'd like to encourage. Not the one that wants to shrink a big stack of unwanted paperwork. The resume is very important: but the reason it's important is that it's a formal documentation of experiences that supports what you've written in your letter. So we're going to deal with the cover letter first.

Most job hunters write cover letters that are concerned with what they want. They ramble on and on about how qualified they are, what kind of position they feel they deserve, and how wonderful their recommendations from their teachers are. Leaving aside for the moment the huge difficulty that all such letters tend to sound the same, ask yourself -- Why does the employer care? What problem of the employer's does such a letter solve? How is he or she going to be convinced that the five minutes it takes to read the letter will be time well spent?

The trick to writing a successful cover letter is to say something that the prospective employer wants to hear, with a direct application to his or her department or the company itself. And you must come straight to the point in doing so. Keep in mind that even if an employer is looking for someone to hire, time is a very valuable commodity. You can't make someone wade through a sheaf of supporting documents, trying to determine which detail is the most important one. You have to make a strong point quickly -- and (ready for the shocker?) that point does not have to be "I want a job!"

If you can entertain or impress the person reading your letter, you will be surprised at how well you will be received when you follow the letter with a phone call. If you bore the reader, or convince him or her that you've frittered away time they could have spent solving pressing problems, you'll get the cold shoulder.

As a general rule, you might try to begin your letter with a reference to an interesting business-related tidbit that pertains to something your reader will recognize immediately as important. If you are faithful about following the relevant trade magazines (or, at the very least, *The Wall Street Journal*) you should have access to some piece of industry news that will stand out. (Even though your future employer is "in the business," he or she may not always have time to keep up with the industry as a whole.) Make a solid impression!

There are several specific formats you can use to write a good letter to a prospective employer. The one you choose will depend upon what the situation is at the time of your contact. Are you just beginning your search and primarily seeking advice? Are you well on your way and looking for more than just a handshake and good wishes? Is there an actual job opening you've found and wish to pursue? Or are you trying to make points with someone you've already spoken with by way of a memorable "thank-you" note?

THE EXPLORATORY LETTER
Use this letter when...

... you are trying to make a contact with an industry professional who can add to your knowledge of the field and/or steer you toward another contact.

The Exploratory Letter is an absolutely essential component of the first phase of your job hunt. You're feeling your way around the job market in an industry, and you're more than likely doing battle with all the negative stereotypes that surround a "newcomer" to the field. Therefore, you must grab the reader's attention from the very first sentence you write. You must make yourself sound like a person worth meeting. You want your reader to stop what he or she is doing and think, "Gee -- here's someone who's a notch or two above the rest. Might make sense to get together with 'em."

Begin with an unusual first paragraph. And by unusual, I mean unusual. Do not begin with the words "I am a..." under any circumstances. No matter what you follow these or similar words with ("senior graduating from Northern South Shore College"; "promising undiscovered novelist"; "former junior vice president of Megacorp International") you'll be talking about your perspective and your needs instead of the employer's. Don't let that happen.

Try something different. For example, suppose you're writing to the Ace Shoelace Company because you are sure there's going to be a big boom in the designer shoelace area. You've been reading Fit To Be Tied, the industry trade magazine, and you've come across a couple of very interesting predictions on this subject by leading shoelace analysts. You've figured out who you should speak with by attending a local trade show and conversing with a friendly Ace sales rep. You might begin your letter like this:

November 30, 1988

Mr. Tyrone Layssus
Marketing Manager
Ace Shoelace Company
Fourteen Wingtip Place
Shoetown, USA 12345

Dear Mr. Layssus

I just read in <u>Fit To Be Tied</u> that the average American owns eight pairs of shoes, six of which require shoelaces. Of those six, five are typically fitted with dull brown laces. It struck me that there might be an interesting career in finding creative ways to market designer shoelaces -- ways that would offer an exciting

27

```
alternative to the consumer and increase
sales at the same time.  I would like to
talk with you about the shoelace industry
and the types of careers you might advise
pursuing.
```

This paragraph conveys to the reader that you have been keeping up with the industry, that you've been thinking about the information you've come across, and that you are coming up with some creative ideas.   (And, by the way, even if your idea is completely off-base -- which is unlikely -- it shows, at the very least, that you are trying.)   All of this sets you apart from the vast majority of applicants. What employer wouldn't even consider talking to the author of the above paragraph?

Not many.   Unfortunately, there are two reasons that you can't just stop here, sign your name, and mail the thing. One is that the person who'll eventually be deciding to hire you may not even be looking at the letter yet: your letter may be read by a personnel officer or a receptionist, and these are people who've probably read more cover letters than any human being should.   Accordingly, they frequently bring a rather jaded approach to things.   So you've got to try harder to stand out for them, which is a tall order.

The other reason is that even if you are talking to the decision-maker, and even if he or she is considering talking to you, you want more than consideration.   You want an appointment.   So your goal is get them to want one, too. Fortunately, you have at least two more paragraphs with which to get your reader to decide that you're worth speaking to in person.

The second paragraph of the Exploratory Letter should explain in more detail why you have chosen that particular industry -- and why you have chosen to get in touch with your reader.   It might go something like this:

```
I first became intrigued by the shoelace
industry a couple of years ago, when the
first designer shoelaces were introduced.
```

I was especially fascinated by the variety
of colors for high-top sneakers. I
happened to mention this to Edward Eyelet,
one of your sales reps, at the recent
<u>American Shoelace Manufacturer's Con-
ference</u> here in Knottsville. He told me
that you knew the fashion shoelace field
quite thoroughly, and suggested that I
contact you.

A couple of warnings are in order here, warnings that
probably shouldn't need to be expressed in the first place,
but fall into the "better-safe-than-sorry" category.   Make sure
you don't say that Mr. Eyelet suggested you get in touch with
your contact unless he actually did.   Make sure not to use
Mr. Eyelet's name in the letter unless you've first cleared it, at
least informally, with Mr. Eyelet (it's a rare professional who
won't be flattered by such a request).   Make sure that you
do know the broad outline of recent developments in the
fashion shoelace field, lest you get caught flat-footed in a
subsequent discussion.

Continue, in the third paragraph, with specific reasons
for a brief discussion with your reader:

I am writing to you because I also learned
from Mr. Eyelet that it is your company
that is responsible for the new holo-
graphic shoelaces that have just hit the
market. It's obvious that your company is
a leader in the industry. Your advice
would be especially valued.

If the first three paragraphs don't get the meeting you're
hoping for, nothing will, so you might as well end the letter in
a fourth paragraph stating your next move.

I would greatly appreciate a half hour of
your time to discuss your industry and the
opportunities in it. I will call your
office on Monday, the sixth of December,
to see about arranging a meeting. Thank
you in advance for your time.

Sincerely,

Abigail J Hunter

Abigail J. Hunter
123 Horseshoe Trail
Knottsville USA 12345
999/555-1212 (days)
615/121-5555 (evenings)

The tone of the Exploratory Letter (and all the letters
you write, for that matter) should be upbeat, energetic, and,
above all, enthusiastic. The letter should make it perfectly
clear that you are seeking advice only. Emphasize that you
want very little of the reader's time. It is difficult for most
people to turn down such a request. Most professionals
(who aren't that many years away from having sought a job
themselves) will look upon their appointment as a welcome
reinforcement of their own self-image, that of a qualified,
competent professional in their field.

It's probably a good idea not to include a resume with
this type of letter. Skeptical? Think about it from the
employer's standpoint. What would you think of a letter
that arrived in your hands with a resume attached? No
matter what was outlined in the letter (which you might not
even read once you noticed the resume) you'd probably
assume the writer wanted a job. And you'd be right. So
you'd "file" the whole thing in your "people-who-want-a-job-
whose-resumes-I-should-review-when-I-get-the-time" folder.

If, on the other hand, you open a letter that arrives
without a resume, it's likely that you'll think of it as part of
your everyday "correspondence." And, if that letter is well-

written, engaging, and obviously composed by someone who knows something of the industry, you might even make a mental note: "I wish I had a copy of this person's resume!" Who knows -- you could add the person's name to the list of people you should get together with and simply ask for a copy. (Stranger things have happened!)

Stand out by not sending your resume... even if you've sent resumes with every piece of job search correspondence you've ever written before. The method may take a little time to get used to, but with the Exploratory Letter, it's the best idea.

Once you understand this technique, you'll see why mass mailings and form letters are strongly discouraged in any job search. They're expensive and time-consuming. They produce very poor results (a 5-10% response rate is considered outstanding). And they could actually undermine your efforts once you catch on to how a real job search is conducted. Employers usually know when they have seen your name twice. If they were not impressed the first time (and they won't be impressed by a form letter), you'll have a tough time impressing them next time around. Take the time. Write fantastic Exploratory Letters. You'll spend your hours more productively and make a far better impression.

THE CHALLENGE LETTER
Use this letter when...

... you are trying to receive consideration for a position from a potential employer (with whom, typically, you have not yet spoken) -- though you are unaware of any specific opening.

This letter will challenge the reader to consider you as a possible candidate for a job. It's not unlike the Exploratory Letter; however, it is more forceful, and it incorporates more of a sales pitch. This is probably the most difficult job search letter to write. You must be well prepared to approach the potential employer. Simply put, you have to figure out why this employer would want to hire you, and to do that you must have as much information as possible before you write the letter. (Again, you may wish to consult the Appendix for tips on research techniques.)

Try to determine the biggest challenges that currently face the employer's company. Is it doing so well that it needs to expand? Is there tough new competition to be faced? Has the firm just experienced a downturn in profits? A hostile takeover? A friendly merger?

Some of this information may be difficult to uncover. If the firm is a publicly held corporation, most of the information can be found in an annual report. If it isn't, you'll have to rely on facts you can gather from other contacts in the industry -- for example, someone with whom you've had an appointment as a result of an Exploratory Letter or met at a trade function.

There are three reasons you'll be needing such detailed information. First, you must impress the reader with your in-depth knowledge of the business. Second, you must show your insight into the problems of the industry. And third, you must win the reader's consideration as a potential employee. If you can accomplish these three things then you will be assured an interview. And even if that interview does not result in a position, take heart. You can still come out a winner. How?

If you can't get a job, get a lead. It's a good rule to keep in mind, and it's not as difficult as it sounds. Good people, believe it or not, are still hard to find. Even if there is no opening at the firm you contact, you can begin a very positive relationship and generate new openings -- or perhaps even create a position for yourself! (It happens more often than you might imagine.)

The Exploratory Letter focused on generating leads -- now that you've moved on to the Challenge Letter, there's no reason on earth to ignore potential leads, even though our objective has changed somewhat.

The Challenge Letter is usually longer than the Exploratory Letter, simply because there's more to say. However, you should try to keep your paragraphs short, each one a single idea or statement.

In the first part of the Challenge Letter, concentrate on the reader's business and your insights into it. Then focus on your qualifications in the second part. Finally, conclude by setting up the possibility of a mutually convenient meeting, and assure the reader that you will make the initial contact.

This letter may, in exceptional circumstances, extend beyond a page; but if it does, be warned: it must still read like a one-pager. In other words, your reader must not even realize that you have written a two-page letter. Your content should be simply too engaging for him or her to even realize its length!

For example, suppose you're still interested in the Ace Shoelace Company. Your Challenge Letter might begin like this:

                        November 30, 1988

Mr. Tyrone Layssus
Marketing Manager
Ace Shoelace Company
Fourteen Wingtip Place
Shoetown, USA   12345

Dear Mr. Layssus:

The shoelace industry has experienced tough times recently because of the tremendous popularity of the velcro closure. The traditional manufacturers have been forced to diversify, and those who were ready for the change have had to retool to meet new demands. It must be one of the most challenging eras in shoelace history.

This paragraph is designed to make the reader ask, "Who on earth is writing this?" That's the question you want to plant, because in order to answer it, your potential employer is going to have to keep reading!

Your second paragraph is going to get the reader even more interested in what you have to say:

> The Ace Shoelace Company has always been the favorite of shoe manufacturers nationwide. Your net profits last year exceeded industry averages by fifteen percent. However, as mentioned in your recent annual report, this was two percent below last year's performance.

Now you've got the reader a little bit on the defensive. That's okay -- in the next paragraph you're going to let him or her feel a whole lot better.

> Net sales, however, are misleading. Reports indicate that your firm incurred major capital expenditures due to a new velcro plant recently completed in Seoul, Korea. Once functional, the new plant will allow you to recapture virtually all of your previous market share for both styles of shoe fasteners.

Now the reader feels great, and is certain that whoever you are, you know your stuff.

Your next paragraph will begin the second portion of the letter, in which you tell the reader something about your qualifications:

> I have followed your company's progress so closely for a very important reason. For the past three years I have been the top sales rep at Sellright Shoes. Your laces and velcro closures have been a crucial

> product benefit in my pitch to retailers.
> The $100,000 gross in my territory alone
> over the last quarter attests to this
> fact.

Finally!   The reader has some idea who you are!   But he or she is probably still on the lookout for even more information.   Give that information out in strategically-placed "chunks" as your next paragraphs continue the "pitch":

> My boss reports that I've done so well in
> selling my product because I know it
> inside and out and can convey an
> appreciation for its quality.   I enjoy my
> work because I believe in what I sell.
>
> I'm writing you because I'm interested in
> taking my sales skills to the shoelace
> industry.   I believe that more shoe
> manufacturers should know about the
> importance of shoelaces.   I was hoping to
> talk with you and get your advice about
> how sales in the shoelace industry work.

What's happened here?   You've exhibited your knowledge of the industry, made an exceptionally strong presentation to the potential employer, and discreetly entered your name in the employer's "mental computer" as an outstanding applicant -- all without using the words *I want a job.*"   Your reader should, by now, be ready to talk.   Show initiative in your last paragraph:

> I will contact your office next Wednesday
> to set up a meeting.   Thank you in advance

for your help and advice. I look forward
to speaking with you.

Sincerely,

Abigail J. Hunter

Abigail J. Hunter
123 Horseshoe Trail
Knottsville USA 12345
999/555-1212 (days)
999/121-5555 (evenings)

Now, after reading that letter, wouldn't you want to meet
you?

There are four important "musts" to keep in mind about
the Challenge Letter.   You must be aggresive, but in a subtle
way: remember how little most people like a "hard sell."
(Use your knowledge as the tool, not bull-headedness.)   You
must never exaggerate your qualifications: doing so will
almost always remove you from serious consideration when
your subterfuge is exposed.   You must always state facts.
And you must always give the reader what he or she is
hoping to read: a letter from an intelligent, well-spoken
professional.

Just let your best qualities come through and you'll find
some very receptive people at the other end when you make
your follow-up phone calls.

THE DIRECT RESPONSE LETTER
Use this letter when....

*... you are aware of a specific job opening and wish to
make a strong positive impression on the person
responsible for filling the position.*

The key word to remember here is "direct."   Get right
to the point, no matter what else you do.

Once again, you should keep the employer's perspective in mind. Let's say someone has gone to the trouble of writing a lengthy job description, and states very clearly in it that a certain job requires typing skills of 45 words per minute. How will that person view a cover letter that goes on and on about how willing an applicant is to work to improve his or her current four-words-a-minute pace? What would you think of such a letter?

Not much. Admit it.

The reader will be looking for responses that come as close as possible to the requirements of the published job description. In both your cover letter and your resume, you must always remember this. (Yes, it is advisable to send a resume with a Direct Response Letter -- we'll explore resume writing techniques in detail in the next chapter.)

Of course, in most cases, the employer will not end up with someone who fits the description *exactly*. Furthermore, employers are frequently somewhat unsure about what is required for a position, due to the departure of an employee with unusual know-how or extensive experience with the firm. In a strict sense, such a person is "irreplaceable;" the next person who holds the post will almost certainly fail to provide the exact set of skills and "gut feelings" for how to get things done in that particular organization.

Keep in mind, too, that you may be writing to a search committee rather than an individual. Search committees usually consist of a group of four or five executives who collectively make hiring recommendations -- the *final* decision, however, is almost always made by a senior member. Having your application reviewed by the search committee is to your advantage. Why? There is a greater chance that you will appeal to at least one of the people on the committee. And if there's a difference of opinion among committee members, there's an excellent chance it will be resolved by scheduling an interview with you. Getting an interview, of course, is the whole idea!

Let's take a look at how the Direct Response Letter works. You've just heard from your friend at the Ace Shoelace Company that there is an opening for a sales manager at Tie-R-Less Shoelace, Inc. You have the name of the contact person because of your top-notch networking efforts. You also have a basic idea of the job description's requirements. The company is looking for someone with a strong sales background, at least five years of experience, three of which must be in the shoelace industry. Finally, you know that Tie-R-Less wants to hire someone within the next three weeks. How do you proceed?

You should begin your first paragraph by mentioning your contact and explaining why you're writing. Make sure this paragraph convinces the reader that you are just the person for the job:

                              November 30, 1988

      Mr. Dwight Doubleknot
      Marketing Manager
      Tie-R-Less Shoes
      Seventeen Wornsole Place
      Toehold, USA   12345

      Dear Mr. Doubleknot:

      Mr. Tyrone Layssus, of the Ace Shoelace
      Co., suggested that I contact you about
      your current need for a sales manager. I
      would be very interested in talking with
      you about this position because I have the
      credentials, creativity, and energy to do
      the job.

Your second paragraph should respond to the unspoken demand the reader will be formulating after that opening paragraph: "Oh, yeah? Prove it." So prove it.

I have been the top sales rep for
Sellright Shoes for the past several years
and I now want to translate my skills to a
management position. My knowledge of the
shoe business is extensive. I know that
the customer is primarily concerned about
price and quality. I have always given my
customers satisfaction in both areas.

At this point the reader may well be ready to call you
in for the interview, but just in case more information
is needed, continue the third paragraph along these
lines:

I received a BA in Economics with honors
in 1984. While in college I spent all my
summers in retail sales working in the
family shoe business. Upon graduation I
soon became the leading sales rep for
Sellright Shoes. The position you offer
appeals to me because you produce the
number two shoelace in the country. I
feel there is no better place for me to
realize my management potential.

Some of this writing is a bit vague. That's fine: you're
writing a sales letter, one that will highlight the points where
you meet the requirements of the job description (in this
case, strong sales background and five years of experience,
three in the shoelace industry) and get you an interview.
You still need to have something to say at the interview!
  Note that in this letter, the applicant may not technically
"meet" the literal requirements for the job, but has done a
good job of putting the best "spin" on the credentials he does
possess -- with an eye to the job description that may be lying
alongside his letter on the reader's desk. The point is to

dazzle the reader with your overall suitability as an industry-wise employee, then throw spotlights on the elements of your background that are in greatest agreement with the description.

Close with the standard promise to take the initiative in contacting your reader:

> I will contact your office next Wednesday to set up a meeting. Many thanks for your time and consideration; I look forward to speaking with you.
>
> Sincerely,
>
> *Abigail J Hunter*
>
> Abigail J. Hunter
> 123 Horseshoe Trail
> Knottsville USA 12345
> 999/555-1212 (days)
> 999/121-5555 (evenings)

The Direct Response Letter should be only three or four paragraphs long -- and never more than one page in length.

THE MORE-THAN-A-THANK-YOU THANK-YOU LETTER
Use this letter when...

... you want to reinforce a strong presentation you gave at an interview, or repair the damage done to your candidacy by a weak one.

It goes without saying that you should write a note to each contact you meet, thanking the person for the time spent away from what is, undoubtedly, a busy schedule. You can, however, use that letter in a dynamic, positive way to sell your strengths as a potential candidate -- either at the contact's firm or elsewhere in the industry.

In most cases, the meetings you have will leave you with new questions, issues, and ideas that you'll want to follow up. The thank-you letter is a perfect opportunity to briefly demonstrate your grasp of any new areas, and outline any fresh perspectives you've gained. In addition, the thank-you letter can be the best means of re-establishing yourself if you're unhappy with the way your meeting went.

Assume, for instance, that you've had your interview with Tie-R-Less Shoelace, and the meeting ended with Mr. Doubleknot saying, "Well, you're a very intersting candidate. Unfortunately, though, we're looking for someone with more shoelace experience." Now you mentioned quite clearly in an earlier letter that you grew up in the shoe business; apparently that didn't leave as strong an impression as you'd hoped. Many applicants would, after the interview, dash off three or four sentences thanking Mr. Doubleknot for his time, then hope that the interview gods would somehow intervene and show the employer the error of his ways. You're writing a letter anyway -- why not give yourself another chance?

Take the time to compose an interesting letter. The one that follows can serve as a good model.

November 30, 1988

Mr. Dwight Doubleknot
Marketing Manager
Tie-R-Less Shoes
Seventeen Wornsole Place
Toehold, USA   33111

Dear Mr. Doubleknot:

Thank you very much for taking the time to
see me the other day. Now more than ever,
I am convinced that Tie-R-Less is a top-
notch operation, one for which I'd like to
work. I realize you're looking for someone
with more shoelace experience, but let me
try to outline briefly exactly why my
background is the best alternative.

My sales experience at Sellright Shoes has
given me a valuable insight to the overall
needs of the shoe and shoelace industries.
I have a good sense of what manufacturers
are looking for in a shoelace, and I know
what the consumer looks for on the retail
end. A good sales manager must be in touch
with the market in order to motivate his
sales force. I not only believe I can do
well, but am also quite confident that I
can contribute significantly to your
company.

I would be happy to meet with you again to
answer any further questions you might
have, and I'd be glad to prepare an outline
of my management strategies, designed

specifically for your company. I realize
how busy things can get around your office;
if I haven't heard from you within a week
or two, I'll call to see if we can set
something up.

Again, thank you very much for your time.

Sincerely,

Abigail J. Hunter

Abigail J. Hunter
123 Horseshoe Trail
Knottsville USA 33111
999/555-1212 (days)
999/121-5555 (evenings)

With any luck, you'll have the employer thinking, "Here's
a person who really wants that job. Hunter seems
competent, energetic, intelligent... maybe I should take
another look at her."

Whether you consider that likely or not, remember: you
have everything to gain and nothing to lose from writing such
a letter.   Even if the answer is still "no," Mr. Doubleknot may
be so impressed by your initiative that he'll recommend you
to someone else in the industry!

WHAT'S NEXT?

Now that you have an idea of the importance of the
different kinds of letters you can write to keep your job
search rolling, it's time to work on creating the perfect
resume. That's what will be tackled in the next chapter.

CHAPTER TWO:
The Resume

YOUR LIFE ON ONE PAGE

Many people expend considerable effort trying to compose the "perfect resume." For many, many job searches, there is simply no such thing.

In today's competitive job market, it is frequently necessary to tailor your resume to each type of job opportunity that comes along. You may find yourself saying, "Come on -- I don't have all year for this. There must be some way to create a single resume that will fit a variety of situations!"

It's true. There are certain kinds of opportunities where most employers will look for broadly similar qualifications. In some cases, one resume might do the trick. The idea of a new resume for each job still has a great deal of validity, though.

Just as you write your cover letters keeping the needs of the potential employer in mind, you must often do the same when drafting your resume. If you come across an opportunity that requires a substantially different set of skills than the one for which your first resume was written, you will need a substantially different resume. It's a lot of work, but it will pay off. Don't despair -- the changes you'll make from resume to resume will probably be minor ones. (By the way, if you have -- or have access to -- a word processor, you'll save quite a lot of time.)

THE FIRST DRAFT

Have you ever cooked a really substantial stew? You start out gathering and preparing a great many ingredients: carrots, beef, turnips, onions, a bay leaf or two, potatoes, tomatoes, some soup stock, spices of your own... you think to yourself that, once it really gets boiling, you'll want to add a pinch of this... a touch of that...

Then you toss all the painstakingly sliced, diced, and chopped pieces into the pot... and guess what?

They don't fit.

All the work it took to prepare those ingredients, and now you're going to have to take some out!

With a resume, what you decide to take out is every bit as important as what you initially want to put in. And if you're just getting started, it's probably tough to know what's important and what isn't in the first place!

With a stew, how would you solve the problem? (Assume that you can't simply go out and buy another pot; there's a nationwide stewpot shortage on.) One way to solve it might be to think of the person you'll be serving at dinner that evening. Does he or she like turnips? No? Get rid of them. How about the celery or the onions?

The first draft is a real luxury because you're the only one who has to "taste the stew" at that point. So toss everything in and then start subtracting!

You will have to work hard to choose the right experiences in your background and fit them on a one-page resume (virtually all professional resumes are one page long.) Know who you're "cooking for" and use that person's standards as your own. You'll find that you've gained some objectivity yourself!

WHERE TO BEGIN

Choosing experiences from your varied background as you write your first draft can be a nightmare. Immediately, all sorts of questions come to mind: How far back should I go? Should I include anything I did in high school? How much of my college experience should I list? Is it worth putting down jobs I did "just to make money?" How about my outside activities?

All these questions are valid and need answers. But do yourself a big favor. Don't answer them at this stage.

Start by making a list of *everything!* Try to think of all the significant events or activities in your life. Don't limit yourself: list jobs, school activities, sports, awards, honors, travel, musical talent, hobbies, foreign language fluency, office skills (such as typing, shorthand, or word processing), and charitable activities -- in short, any and every skill, interest, or worthy achievement that might be of interest to an employer. Make a point of filling up several pages. (Some employer somewhere will be thrilled to learn that you play the tuba and speak Farsi. Put it all down.)

There are a number of objectives behind this process. One is to build your confidence. Most people forget about all the things they have accomplished in life and concentrate on their mistakes or misfortunes. Another is to help clarify in your own mind exactly what it is that you like to do and are good at doing. Finally, you must establish a list of your accomplishments for your own reference; you'll be mentioning these heroic deeds prominently throughout your job search process!

Some of the items on your list may not be appropriate for inclusion on your resume; however, the simple act of classifying these items can create patterns that will, in turn, remind you of certain career strengths you may have overlooked. If you won a Good Citizenship Award in high school, and later volunteered to head the local Meals-on-Wheels program after graduating from college, both of these activities would be important indicators of your leadership qualities and vision of community service, and should be included in your "long list." However, when undertaking a later draft of your resume, you might include only the volunteer work on the grounds that it best exemplified the accumulated skills on your list.

Once you have listed everything, you will be ready to take on the task of selecting those items you feel will present the best picture to your potential employer.

THE BASICS – AND BEYOND

There are certain basic elements that should appear in every resume. For example, there should be standard sections that outline your education and work experience.

In the education section, be sure to list the highest degree or certificate that you have attained. If you have been out of college for a few years, all you really need to list is your college experience. However, if you're still in college, it may be appropriate to list your high school. Don't forget to list any summer courses you may have taken, or any post-graduate training you may have. Your reader will be interested in your pattern of self improvement. You may also want to mention significant awards and prizes. If you won any national awards, or were a finalist or winner of a relevant competition, outline these as well. Give some thought to all the educational experiences you've had, and list those that seem to you to be most significant. As with all the items on your resume, list the most recent ones first and work backwards. Once again: how do you know if an item is worth including? Think of what your potential employer would most like to read.

When listing your work experiences, think carefully about which are best suited for the industry or job for which you are applying. It may be possible to present your experience so that it focuses directly on the kinds of skills and talents for which the employer is looking. If you are applying for a sales job, for example, and have worked at two or three jobs that involved sales, it may be a good idea to list them separately in a section called "Sales Experience." You would then list the other jobs you've had in a section called "Other Experience." This method gives you the flexibility to arrange your experience out of chronological order if need be. In this way, you are doing the sorting for the employer. He or she can look at your resume and immediately see that you are thinking about the reader's needs because you have listed the most relevant facts first.

Avoid at all costs making the reader look over your resume, focus upon the wrong job (perhaps the first one listed) and asking, "What on earth does this person want to do?"

At this point, it's a good idea to examine the idea of placing a "job objective" at the head of your resume. This is the line that you see at the top of many resumes that says something like, "Professional Goal: Become the top shoelace salesperson in the Northeast." You might assume that because you go to the trouble to say that you want to be a salesperson, you will be assumed to have the qualifications. The fact is, virtually every employer will look immediately beyond the objective you state for the experience to back it up. If he or she can't find it right away, the assumption will be that the top line of your resume is less objective than pipe-dream.

In other words, don't bother with a job objective. Remember that your letter is the primary place to communicate your goals. Make your resume the place that clearly outlines your background.

Once you determine which of your work experiences is most relevant, list some of your related skills -- ones that might not fit into either of the two categories mentioned above. For example, if you have any fluency in foreign languages, or computer-related abilities (such as some knowledge of programming), be sure to list these in separate sections... as long as they're relevant to the job you're seeking.

In some cases it will be important to list travel experiences. If your target employer has any international or nationwide interests, both travel and language background will be essential.

At the bottom of your resume, it is usually appropriate to list some of your activities outside of your work or school life. Employers want people they like working for them. And even if your interests are not the same as your employer's, you may have some unusual interest that adds a new dimension to your candidacy.

"REFERENCES AVAILABLE
UPON REQUEST"

Should you bother inviting the employer to inquire after your references on your resume? Only if you have extra room.   Otherwise, don't worry about it.   Most employers will expect you to have some kind of recommendation from a previous supervisor, associate, or instructor.   Advertising the fact that yours are available for review only affirms a fact your reader is probably already taking for granted.

Whether or not you specify anything about the matter on your resume, it's an excellent idea to prepare a separate sheet that contains the names, addresses, and phone numbers of your references.   Bring this sheet with you to any interviews you schedule.   If the potential employer asks for references, you're ready.

A variety of related questions surround the issue of references for potential employers.   Who should write the recommendation?   What if you don't know anyone within the industry?   Suppose you can't ask your boss because you don't want to reveal the fact that you're engaged in a job search?   Should you ask a prominent figure in an industry to write a reference -- someone with only limited knowledge of your experiences?   Should you settle for recommendations that are less than ecstatic in their descriptions of you?

If you've recently graduated from college, the best person to ask for a reference might be a professor you've studied with closely, or a supervisor from a work-study program, summer job, or internship.   Ideally, the person most familiar with your work should write your primary recommendation -- and for most job seekers, this individual is a supervisor or department head. An excellent recommendation from your current employer is usually the best referral you can get.   One way to avoid tipping off your boss to your job search is to ask for written summaries at each performance review.   Keep these on file.   You never know when you may need this paperwork, and maintaining accurate records of your progress within the company can allow you to avoid having to ask for a reference at a sensitive time.   When you do get around to seriously conducting your job search, the summary may not be completely up-to-date, but it will reflect the good feelings of your supervisor.

If you just plain don't like your current job, and can't depend on a positive recommendation because your boss doesn't like you, it's obvious that you'll have to look elsewhere. Consider asking for a reference from a colleague at your level in the company you presently work for, or in a similar position at another organization. The more familiar the individual is with your work, the better.

You might also want to ask a satisfied client or customer you've worked with successfully to write out his or her impressions of your work. A happy customer endorsement is sometimes even better than a glowing letter from your boss. Whenever you have the chance to add such a recommendation to your file, do so -- even if you aren't currently looking for a new job.

It is always a good idea to have one reference on file from a person not associated with your work, thereby supplying your prospective employer with an additional perspective on your personality. Recommendations from a leader of a community group, a professor you've kept in regular contact with, or even a close friend with some professional credentials, would all be good candidates for inclusion in your portfolio.

Letters of recommendation are not always necessary, but can be quite useful. Many job seekers prefer to maintain a list of references "on call" -- that is, available for a quick phone conversation with a potential employer. A personal phone call can carry a great deal more weight than a vague, all-purpose summation of your capabilities.

One important note: be sure to keep your "recom-menders" informed of your plans. If it's been some time since you last used a recommendation, drop a copy of your resume and a photocopy of the original letter in the mail, addressed to the person who wrote the reference. Be sure you have permission from the proper person before using any recommendation.

Three references are plenty. Often, two will suffice. Most employers will go to the trouble of phoning your references only after having made a decision to consider you seriously for a position, and will probably do so in an effort to reinforce their positive impressions. Be sure that these impressions will be reinforced. Don't rely on people whose opinion of you is less than clear, even if they carry considerable weight within the industry you're trying to enter. Using an industry "bigwig" as a reference will only help if you know the person in question fairly well. Try to elicit recommendations from people who can honestly speak highly of your background, attitude toward your work, and overall character.

CONTENT

Once you've developed guidelines that will give you some idea of the kinds of experiences you should list in your resume, you need to know how each experience should be described. Most employers look for dynamic people who take initiative, demonstrate leadership, and get the job done.

If what readers are looking for is dynamism, be dynamic! Any descriptions of jobs, activities, interests, or achievements should be phrased in an active way. Try to reflect the very results you are outlining in your writing style.

For example, suppose you had written this book, and were looking for another writing assignment. How would you phrase the line in your resume that describes your experience with *The Job Search Handbook?* Perhaps you'd try something along these lines:

Wrote book on job hunting techniques.

Responsible for writing 144-page book entitled The Job Search Handbook.

Took assignment to write a book about job search strategies.

All of these statements are true -- but are they *effective?*

Think about your targets. What do they want to know? They're probably interested in hiring someone to complete a specific writing assignment. They have a deadline in mind. They have an idea of what the book should be about, and, naturally, they want the book to be as well-written as possible. Odds are that they don't want to pay top dollar, either, though they expect some experience. (Some of these requirements may actually show up in the job description -- for others you will have to read "between the lines.")

Now: how do the three resume examples we've come up with address the employer's criteria as we've identified them? The fact is, not one of them does so convincingly. So you "wrote" something. Who cares? If you can't "write," there's not a heck of a lot you can offer as a freelancer in the first place. So you were "responsible" for a "144-page book." What information does that give the employer than he or she didn't have   before picking up your resume?   Was the book ever published?   Was it finished on time?   Was it well received?   So you "took" an assignment.   So what?   All the employer knows is that you didn't actually refuse your last project -- and that's not much to go on!

After establishing exactly what the employer is looking for, you can write a much better summation of your accomplishments, and make yourself sound like a bit of an overachiever at the same time:

> *Researched and wrote, under strict deadline, comprehensive, well-received, trade quality hand-book for job hunters.*

This description, which begins with two powerhouse verbs and continues with straightforward, discrete chunks of relevant information, is more of what you (and the employer) want.

Take a close look at that sentence one more time. You'll notice that it begins to get at some of the issues in which the employer has an interest. (It also avoids mentioning how much you were paid for the project.   This is generally a good idea.)

Remember, your goal is to get as close to "top dollar" for your efforts as you can.   Whether you're freelancing or looking for a full-time job, it goes without saying that you want to be in the best possible position once it comes time to discuss salary.   One good way to make your accomplishments stand out is to use an active, specific grammatical style.   (Which sounds better: "Was named to post requiring me to edit and supervise class yearbook", or "Edited class yearbook and supervised staff of twelve"?)

Use descriptive language. Wherever possible, put some kind of relative dimension on the work you have done. How much money did you raise? How many books did you sell? Did you lead a ten-member or 1000-member tour? Did you graduate fifth in your class, and if so, was that five out of 500 or five out of six?

Give your potential employer a yardstick by which to measure your accomplishments. That way, you may even outshine someone with a more impressive record who neglects to describe their background effectively!

However, make sure you're using a 36-inch yardstick and not a two-inch model. It bears repeating: keep in mind that you must always state truths. You're trying to create a document that sells your virtues, but don't get carried away. If you worked on just part of a project, don't take credit for all of it. If you waited on tables, don't say you were a restaurant manager. Truth in advertising -- and that really is the field you've entered into here -- is an absolute must.

It goes without saying that your resume should be proofread meticulously. One spelling error or typo can automatically eliminate you from consideration for a position. Keep in mind that along with your cover letter, your resume is one of your most important writing samples. It's a pretty clear indicator of how well you communicate. If you miss a typo, your reader may think, "Maybe this person will miss important details while on the job, too." Get a friend or an objective third party to read your resume after you've proofed it. A new eye can often pick up an obvious error that you've missed. Remember that over time you may well lose the ability to look clearly at something you've been working on intensely.

You needn't worry about producing a resume that looks like a Cadillac when a Chevy will do the trick. Some people believe that top-notch design and typesetting is always necessary to make the right impression, but unless you're applying for a position as a graphic artist or design professional it's generally not the case. Most employers look at how each resume describes a person who could fill their needs; as a rule, they couldn't care less about whether the thing is set in Futura, Times Roman, Bodoni -- or on your word processor or quality typewriter, for that matter. Of course, a well-designed and pleasant-looking resume is easier to read than one that looks like a second cousin to a ransom note. The fact remains, however, that it's not, in the final analysis, how your resume looks that really matters -- it's what it says.

Your resume should, at any rate, end up on good-quality bond paper. It should be produced by a photocopier with virtually no distortion or streaking, or, if it's in your budget, by a laser printer or offset press service. Your goal is a consistent level of reproduction quality from resume to resume.

It's usually wise to be somewhat conservative when it comes to selecting a color for your resume. Accepted colors include white, beige, and grey. You begin to take chances if you opt for any other color.

Keep the size standard: 8 1/2" x 11". Legal size may stick out in a pile, but it will also get a lot more abuse, and an odd-sized resume may get thrown out by a meticulous employer who doesn't like loose ends.

When you create your master copy, use a good quality typewriter or computer printer that offers "letter quality" output. Stay away from smudgy typewriter ribbons, and (even worse) dot-matrix printers, which reproduce with horrific results. Your final reader may be looking at a copy of a copy of a copy!

Because you may be creating a few different versions of your resume, it may be a good idea to look into preparing your resume on a computer, as this allows for very easy editing. Most cities and towns have word processing services that provide machines for self-service or low-cost resume preparation by a professional. Make sure you use a service that will keep your resume on file. Of course, if you have or have access to a personal computer and a high-quality printer, you may be able to do the job yourself!

To illustrate the idea of tailoring a resume to fit an employer's needs, three different samples follow -- using the same job seeker's background.

THE CHRONOLOGICAL RESUME
Use this resume when...

... most of your experience relates directly to the position or industry that is the focus of your search.
Abigail J. (for Job) Hunter has created a resume that, in a clear, straightforward, and concise manner, covers the basics of her experience. In this example, Abigail wants to enter the shoe industry in a management capacity. Accordingly, the reader's eye is drawn immediately to the upper left hand corner of the page, where the description of her most important experiences relative to a career in that field can be found.

On a quick scan (which is all you can count on your resume receiving), the next area that demands the reader's attention is the "education" section, with Abigail's summer business seminar listed first. Again, she has prominently positioned the most relevant item to entry into the industry as a manager: the summer business seminar courses in management and marketing.

Notice that the descriptions of her various positions are written in an abbreviated style. This allows Abigail not only to give the impression that she understands that the reader's time is valuable, but also to use concise, active phrases to strengthen the impact of each idea: *top sales rep; served customers; supervised; performed.*

Abigail's resume has been set in an attractive, easy-to-read typeface (Times Roman), although a word processor's standard typewriter face (such as Courier), could have been substituted without any real change in the overall professional appearance. The resume has plenty of white space, does not appear to overwhelm the reader with facts, and is confined to one page.

ABIGAIL J. HUNTER
123 Horseshoe Trail
Knottsville, USA 12345
Work: 999/555-1212
Home: 999/121-5555

EXPERIENCE

Sellright Shoes, Lasting, USA
Sales Representative. Top sales rep for this multi-million dollar shoe manufacturer. Only rep in northeast territory, including New York and New England. Set new sales records ($400,000+ in 1988). Winner of three Golden Sole Awards. 1985 to present.

Sole Mates, Heelville, USA
Assistant Manager. Supervised sales staff, performed sales duties, maintained inventory and daily receipts, for this million dollar shoe retailer. Managed store while manager was on vacation. Summer 1984.

The Feet Treat, Comfort, USA
Sales Clerk. Served customers by fitting and selecting shoe sizes and styles. Assisted manager in keeping inventory and accounting.
Summer 1983.

Shoemaker's Landscaping, Greenage, USA
Mechanic and Groundskeeper. Maintained all lawn care equipment and assisted architect in this small landscaping firm. Summer 1982.

The Bagel Bakery, Doughville, USA
Assistant Baker. Served customers, assisted baker in daily food preparations. Summer 1981.

EDUCATION

Werton Summer Business Seminar, Philly, USA
Courses in management and marketing. Summer 1987.

Impressive University, Learnedville, USA
B.A. in History with honors, June 1985.

The Honorable Local High School, Shoetown, USA
Honors graduate, June 1981.

Activities
Impressive U. Student Government - Chair of Business Committee
Thomas McCan Dorm Supervisor
Meals-on Wheels Volunteer

SKILLS: Word Processing(El Word), database(ZBaseX), and spreadsheet(Loti).

LANGUAGES: Fluent in Modern Greek and Italian.

TRAVEL: Greece, Italy, Northeast U.S.

MEMBERSHIPS: Vice President of Knottsville Investment Club
Knottsville PTA.

PERSONAL: Avid tennis player, piano, skiing.

References available upon request.

THE FUNCTIONAL RESUME
Use this resume when...

... you have little directly related experience in your target field, and wish to focus attention on the skills you have developed rather than the jobs you've held.

With a functional resume, Abigail is able to distill her experiences into a format that best presents her background as it relates to the job she's trying to get -- in this case, a sales-related one. Note that this resume is of particular interest to an employer in the shoe industry, but demonstrates achievements relevant to virtually any company with a sales force.

Acting on the indications she's received from her research, Abigail has highlighted her experiences in sales, management, and communications, and has emphasized skills rather than paying jobs. This decision has resulted in a bit more space to expand on her experiences, while still allowing the resume to retain an uncluttered appearance.

This style does have one potential drawback: the reader may become frustrated if he or she has difficulty determining exactly *how* you gained the skills you specify. Wherever possible, support your claims with pertinent details.

ABIGAIL J. HUNTER
123 Horseshoe Trail
Knottsville, USA 12345
Work: 999/555-1212
Home: 999/121-5555

SALES

Proven sales effectiveness: top sales representative with a record $400,000+ in 1988 (increase of 20% from 1987). Territory in competitive New York-New England markets. Contacts with more than 250 retail outlets. Manufacturing and retail experience. Winner of three company sales awards.

MANAGEMENT

Leadership skills: Supervised 8-member sales staff for million- dollar retailer. Assumed full managerial responsibilities for vacation periods. Accounting, inventory, and fullfillment experience. Chair of Student Government Business Committee. Thomas McCan Hall Proctor, 250 student dormitory.

COMMUNICATIONS

Fluent in Modern Greek and Italian. *Travelled* throughout Greece, Italy, Northeast U.S. visiting shoe manufacturers. *Computer Skills:* Word Processing(El Word), database(ZBaseX), and spreadsheet(Loti).

EMPLOYMENT HISTORY

Sellright Shoes, Lasting, USA. Sales Representative. 1985 to present.
Sole Mates, Heelville, USA. Assistant Manager. Summer 1984.
The Feet Treat, Comfort, USASales Clerk. Summer 1983.
Shocmaker's Landscaping, Greenage, USA. Mechanic/Groundskeeper. Summer 1982.
The Bagel Bakery, Doughville, USA. Assistant Baker. Summer 1981.

EDUCATION

Werton Summer Business Seminar, Philly, USA
Courses in management and marketing. Summer 1987.

Impressive University, Learnedville, USA
B.A. in History with honors, June 1985.

The Honorable Local High School, Shoetown, USA
Honors graduate, June 1981.

MEMBERSHIPS

Vice President of Knottsville Investment Club
Knottsville PTA.

PERSONAL

Avid tennis player, piano, skiing.

References available upon request.

THE INDUSTRY-TARGETED RESUME
Use this resume when...

... you have identified specific industry experience required for a job, and wish to demonstrate that you have experience that is identical or closely related.

Abigail has learned of a position in the operations department of a major national shoe firm that requires some management background, familiarity with the retail shoe market, and two to four years of sales or related consumer-sensitive experience. While she does not bring a perfect "package" to the job (having never held a full management position), her resume does highlight the strong points of contact between her record and the formal description.

This resume, which combines aspects of both the chronological and functional resumes, should be used whenever possible. *It is possible that fifteen uses of this resume in your job search will result in your generating fifteen different resumes.* Even though there is a degree of effort in designing these "customized" resumes, doing so is usually well worth the trouble.

An industry-targeted resume presents your experience in the same order that the employer is hoping to find it. It helps the reader by outlining the experience most important to the job description first, and labels the pertinent elements of your background appropriately. In addition, this resume format gives you the flexibility to deemphasize jobs that don't help your candidacy, and strengthen the more relevant items by adding descriptive material targeted to a specific opening.

If you wish to broaden the resume's audience by adding more than one experience section, do so, but beware of diluting the document's impact. This style's appeal is mainly in its direct appeal to employer needs.

ABIGAIL J. HUNTER
123 Horseshoe Trail
Knottsville, USA 12345
Work: 999/555-1212
Home: 999/121-5555

SHOE INDUSTRY EXPERIENCE

Sellright Shoes, Lasting, USA
Sales Representative. Top sales rep for this multi-million dollar shoe manufacturer. Only rep in northeast territory, including New York and New England. Set new sales records ($400,000+ in 1988). Winner of three Golden Sole Awards. 1985 to present.

Sole Mates, Heelville, USA
Assistant Manager. Supervised sales staff, performed sales duties, maintained inventory and daily receipts, for this million dollar shoe retailer. Managed store while manager was on vacation. Summer 1984.

The Feet Treat, Comfort, USA
Sales Clerk. Served customers by fitting and selecting shoe sizes and styles. Assisted manager in keeping inventory and accounting. Summer 1983.

LANGUAGES & TRAVEL

Fluent in Modern Greek and Italian. Travelled throughout Greece, Italy, Northeast U.S. visiting shoe manufacturers.

PREVIOUS EXPERIENCE

Shoemaker's Landscaping, Greenage, USA. Mechanic/Groundskeeper. Summer 1982.
The Bagel Bakery, Doughville, USA. Assistant Baker. Summer 1981.

EDUCATION

Werton Summer Business Seminar, Philly, USA
Courses in management and marketing. Summer 1987.

Impressive University, Learnedville, USA
B.A. in History with honors, June 1985.

The Honorable Local High School, Shoetown, USA
Honors graduate, June 1981.

ACTIVITIES
Impressive U. Student Government - Chair of Business Committee
Thomas McCan Dorm Supervisor
Meals-on Wheels Volunteer

SKILLS

Word Processing(El Word), database(ZBaseX), and spreadsheet(Loti).

MEMBERSHIPS

Vice President of Knottsville Investment Club
Knottsville PTA.

PERSONAL

Avid tennis player, piano, skiing.

References available upon request.

THE AVOID-AT-ALL-COSTS RESUME
Don't ever use this resume.

This resume features a number of serious flaws you should avoid.

To begin with the most obvious drawback this document presents, always use a good quality typewriter or computer printer for the final copy of your resume. The example shown here was obviously set on a circa-1933 yard sale special. Equally important is the resume's content. Do not include your "vital statistics" in any resume (who cares?) and do not highlight the job objective with artsy "tricks" that will distract your reader -- particularly if the objective is a meaningless one. (As we've learned, the objective itself is something of a dispensable item anyway.)

Notice any telephone numbers on the Avoid-At-All-Costs specimen? Neither will the employer in the unlikely event that he or she wishes to contact the author. The employer *will* notice, however, the sloppy typing and proofreading. What *else* is there to notice at the very top of the resume? Let's see. Abigail, it would appear, skis. Abigail plays the piano. Abigal plays tennis. See Abigail ski, play the piano, and play tennis. See Abigail lose the job.

Once you've been out of college for two or three years, "Education" should be listed after work experience and in reverse chronological order. Listing your activities is fine, but why not specify when each activity occurred? Is Abigail *still* a candy-striper? Maybe. Maybe not. Why was candy-stripe work an important experience? Maybe the employer will try to work that question out. Then again... maybe not. *Don't expect the reader to deduce anything.*

Of course, the resume fails spectacularly in its selection and presentation of topics from beginning to end, not merely in the "Activities" section. In the summary of previous positions, the most recent of Abigail's positions appears last, while the ancient history is served up as Item Number One. Few of the details of Abigail's professional background are provided, and the tangibles that do appear are of only marginal interest. The headings are no help, either. "Work History," a cumbersome and weak phrase, might be replaced with the more straightforward "Experience."

Abigail J. Hunter

123 Horseshoe Trail   Height: 5'7"   Weight: 125½
Knottsville, USA 12345   Health: Excellent Born: 11/7/68

```
┌─────────────────────────────────────────────────────────┐
│                     Job Objective                        │
│  To find a management position in the shoelace industry  │
│  or other position in other industry.                    │
└─────────────────────────────────────────────────────────┘
```

Personal
Tennis, piano, skiing

Education
The Honorable Local High School, Shoetown, USA
Honors Graduate, June 1981.

Impressive University, Learnedville, USA
Honors Graduate, June 1985.

Activities
Candy Striper-Shoetown Hospital
Meals-on-Wheels Volunteer
Dorm Supervisor in college
Member of Student Government - Business Committee Chair
Member Knottsville PTA
Member Knottsville Investment Club

Work History
Worker, The Bagel Bakery   Summer 1981
Helper, Shoemaker's Landscaping   Summer 1982
Sales Clerk, The Feet Treat   Summer 1983
Assistant Manager, Sole Mates   Summer 1984
Sales Rep., Sellright Shoes 1985-present

Skills
Word Processing, database, spreadsheet

Languages
Greek and Italian

Travel
Eorope and US

References available upon request.

CHAPTER THREE:
Making Contact

PERSON TO PERSON

Up to this point in your job search, you haven't actually had to make any kind of personal contact with potential employers. While you may have spoken informally with various industry people at trade fairs or on the phone, when it comes to people with hiring authority, you've written some letters. That's about it. Now comes the interesting part.

Now you must speak to a potential employer on the phone or in person during a meeting or interview. That's what this chapter is all about: making contact in person.

By the way, if you're setting up an informational interview on the telephone after sending an Exploratory Letter, you'll find that a great many of the principles outlined in this chapter will apply quite readily to your call. Just remember the terms you stated in your letter, and remember that one of the primary reasons your reader will be willing to meet with you is that *you aren't looking for a job.*

THE PHONE CALL

The first challenge is the phone call. Suppose you've sent off a dozen fantastic letters and are now making the follow-up calls to arrange meetings. Don't simply pick up the phone and ask to speak to Mr. Eyelet, your contact. Prepare for the call.

Before you make your first call, it's a good idea to have a copy of your letter in front of you -- just in case you need to refer to it or reinforce some important fact. It is very likely that your reader will not recall getting your letter.

Another item essential to good calling is a calendar. If you are successful in convincing the person at the end of the line that you're worth calling, be ready to make an appointment! You'd be surprised at the number of people who get to the final stages of the calling process and are then unable to commit to a date. (Having a calendar handy doesn't hurt your image as a well-organized professional, either.)

Be sure as well to have a copy of your resume close at hand. When under pressure, you'll sometimes forget the most important details of your background. With this in mind, you may want to write yourself an outline for the call.

"OH NO!" you may think, "NOT A SCRIPT!" No; don't write out a word-for-word recitation to be delivered in a flat monotone. Jot down some of the key points you'd like to cover in the call, bearing in mind that the phone calls you make should be brief ones. Your intention is to establish friendly contact, get the contact to acknowledge receipt of your letter, make an appointment, and then get off the line. Such a conversation need not last more than three or four minutes.

Now: on to the dynamics of the call itself. Your contact may see the call as an opportunity to screen your qualifications. If he or she can uncover unacceptable elements in your background or presentation, it will be possible to save the time it would take to talk to you in person. This must be avoided at all costs. It is easy to forget someone you've spoken to on the phone; it's much harder to forget someone you've seen in person. If you sense that you are being screened, you must tactfully emphasize the fact that you can only do justice to your qualifications in person, and then ask to meet. If the person insists on reviewing your qualifications, at least you'll be prepared to talk intelligently -- your letter and resume will be right in front of you.

THE SECRETARY

Actually, there are usually *two* people you will have to deal with for each call you make. One, of course, is the contact; the other is the person who's been hired to keep you from getting through!

The contact's secretary or assistant will, alas, often try to screen calls.   You must develop a strategy for getting around these people.   And here's the real challenge: you must do so without making an enemy!

Let's take a look at how a typical encounter with a secretary might go:

> *Switchboard:* Hello, this is Ace Shoelace -- once you buy 'em, you'll wanna tie 'em. How may I help you?
>
> *You:* Ms. Tyman's office, please.
>
> *Switchboard:* Hold on, I'll connect you.
>
> *(Click. Buzz.)*
>
> *Secretary:* Ms. Tyman's office, this is Mr. Nibs speaking.
>
> *You:* Hello, may I please speak with Ms. Tyman?
>
> *Secretary:* Oh, I'm afraid she's in a meeting all morning. May I take a message?

How many times has that happened to you?   You know the story.   If you leave your message, you'll never get a return phone call;   if you persist by calling again and again, you run the risk of alienating both Mr. Nibs, the secretary, and Ms. Tyman, the boss.

There are two obvious (and time-tested) approaches you can take.   First, you can try asking when a good time to call back might be.   Sometimes the secretary will tell you when the meeting (if there really is one) should be over.   With any luck, you can either force the secretary to pinpoint a time when the boss will be available -- or give you some clue as to whether or not you're getting a snow job.

Another strategy is to call when the secretary is not likely to be around.   If you call just before or after regular business hours -- or during lunch -- you may get the boss directly.   (Many salespeople sidestep the "secretary problem" by focusing their calling hours during the periods before 9 a.m. and after 5 p.m.)

Suppose, though, that you reach a secretary who is willing to acknowledge the contact's presence in the office -- but unwilling to let you through until you clearly establish yourself as a Person Who Will Not Waste The Boss's Time. That exchange usually begins something like this:

You: May I please speak with Ms. Tyman?

Secretary: May I ask who is calling?

You: Yes, this is Abigail Hunter.

Secretary: And what is this in regard to?

Now what? If you say that you're calling to get information about careers and/or specific job openings, you'll be catapulted into the dusky limbo of eternal hold. If you make up some "little white lie" (i.e., "It's his sister-in-law Abigail") you'll probably end up embarrassing yourself in front of the secretary and the contact -- and running a pretty good chance of permanently destroying your chances for employment at the firm. The simplest way to parry this question is to respond with something like this:

You: It's in regard to my letter of December fifth.

This way you are being pleasant to the secretary, telling the truth, and ensuring that your intentions are not given away to the wrong person.

But what if the secretary responds with:

Secretary: Well, Ms. Tyman receives a lot of correspondence, sir. Could you tell me the purpose of your call?

Ugh! The stakes get higher! Your best bet now is to take a deep breath and ask yourself honestly whether or not you consider your job search something personal in nature. Sure you do.

You: Actually, Mr. Nibs, it's something of a personal matter that I really should address only to

Ms. Tyman.

With a bit of luck, you've managed to change the secretary's underlying question from "Who is this?" to "Oh, my God, someone's come down with rickets; why am I giving this person such a hard time?" The average secretary will not run the risk of offending a friend of the boss's or prying into personal business. (But beware: if this technique works, be ready for a somewhat puzzled first few seconds when the boss picks up the phone after having been paged for a "personal" call.)

If all else fails, and you end up with a genuine, implacable, iron-fisted guardian of the corporate gates...

> **Secretary:** *I'm sorry, sir, Ms. Tyman has requested that I determine the purpose of her calls before I forward them. May I please tell her the reason for your call?*

... then you'll have to come clean and respond with something that marginally resembles real information:

> **You:** *Certainly. I'm calling Ms. Tyman with regard to getting some data about the shoelace industry. She should recall my letter of last week.*

THE BOSS

At some point during that elaborate phone-dance ritual with the secretary, you will have (one hopes) gotten through to the boss. What do you say now?

Remember your goal: to make an appointment and get off the phone as quickly as possible. Let's see how it might work.

> **Boss:** *Hello, this is Ms. Tyman.*

> **You:** *Ms. Tyman, this is Abigail Hunter; I'm following up my letter of December fifth. I don't*

73

> *know whether or not you recall, but I wrote you that letter outlining my interest in the shoelace industry. I was hoping to set up a brief interview with you to get your advice. (OR: I was hoping to set up a brief interview with you to discuss opportunites at your company.)*

Here's where you find out whether or not your contact reads the mail.

Now it is possible that this alone will be enough to ring a bell, remind the contact of your letter, and motivate Ms. Tyman to schedule you for an interview. But no matter how fantastic your letter was, you should probably be prepared for some kind of dodge at this point:

> **Boss:** *Well, I'm not sure I can help you that much. What kinds of questions did you have? Perhaps I can answer them over the phone. (OR: I tell you what you ought to do. Why don't you send a resume out to me and I'll get back in touch with you after I've reviewed it?)*

These and similar responses -- and there are an infinite number of variations -- bring you to one compelling question: How do you get in the office?

Here are a couple of suggestions. One way is to ask some prepared questions about the shoelace industry that showcase your knowledge of the field. This may jog the contact's memory of your stellar letter and get the conversation moving along a little more smoothly. Another tactic is to emphasize precisely why you feel your contact (and/or the contact's company) has a lot to offer, and how you'd really appreciate a meeting in person to discuss what you have to offer the firm and/or careers in the field.

Finally, if you have not had any luck with these approaches, you can thank the person for his or her time and ask for the name of anyone else who might be helpful. (Remember, if you can't get a job, get a lead.) By all means, be considerate of your contact's time, and do everything you can to keep the conversation short, businesslike, and free from "polarizing" exchanges like this one:

> *Boss: Gee, unfortunately we're in a hiring freeze right now.   Even if I could talk to you, my schedule is absolutely insane this month.   Maybe if you gave us a call back in the spring...*
>
> *You: I have Monday at three open. How's Monday at three?*
>
> *(Pause.)*
>
> *Boss: Um...*
>
> *You: I'm really great, Ms. Tyman. I came in second in my high school's senior debating contest. What do you say? How's Monday at three?*
>
> *(Click.)*
>
> *You: Hello?*

How on earth can you expect to generate a referral from a phone conversation like that?   Why would Ms. Tyman wish such a candidate on her worst enemy?

Far preferable to the above exchange is something like this:

> *Boss: Gee, unfortunately we're in a hiring freeze right now.   Even if I could talk to you, my schedule is insane this month.   Maybe if you gave us a call back in the spring...*
>
> *You: No problem, that's an excellent idea. While I have you on the line, Ms. Tyman, do you mind my asking if there's anyone else in the shoelace field I should contact along these lines?*
>
> *Boss: Oh, let's see... yeah, why don't you give Julie Velcro a call at Knottsville Shoelace.   Hold on, I'll get her number for you.*

What a difference!   Now, instead of a notebook with the

name "Lucy Tyman" scratched out violently, you've got the chance to pursue another lead. And not only that -- now you can begin your letters and phone conversations with, "Ms. Lucy Tyman at Ace shoelace suggested that I..."

ALL ABOUT INTERVIEWS

Suppose that you've finally arranged an interview. Whether you're looking for information about the shoelace industry or for a specific job at Ace Shoelace, you'll need to make certain kinds of preparations for the meeting to be a fruitful one.

Obviously, the preparation for each type of interview will differ. Your goals for each are completely distinct. In the first type, which we'll call the Information Only Interview, you have no knowledge of a specific opening and are hoping to generate new leads and add to your information base. In the second type, which we'll call the Job Interview, you've set an appointment through a referral or a "cold" telephone call to discuss a specific opening for which you feel qualified.

In this chapter we'll examine each type of interview in some detail

THE INFORMATION ONLY INTERVIEW

The best advice for this type of interview is that you should never ask for a job. Be true to your word. You stated in your cover letter that you're seeking advice. Seek advice. Don't worry: no self-respecting employer will let you slip away if you meet the qualifications for a certain position and fulfill the overall needs of the company.

Avoiding the job issue is important; a very different (and probably quite pleasant) mood will prevail in your meeting if the question of employment is not on the agenda. Instead of the employer dreading the point in the interview where he or she will have to disappoint you, contacts can talk about themselves and their own career development. This is informative and should not be underestimated as an "input" to your potential career path, even at a later period in your job search. In addition, your contact will have the opportunity to reflect on the difficulty of finding a job -- both in his or her past and in your current situation. Once this occurs, you'll be seen in a very sympathetic light. But the key is to allow the contact to reach that point without your prodding for immediate results.

You'll also have the opportunity to show off your qualifications. Don't attempt to "sell" yourself directly as a candidate -- but do show how much research you've done, and mention the significant accomplishments in your background if you can do so in a non-threatening way. Doing so will speak volumes about your suitability as a candidate, and will avoid putting your contact on the defensive.

Be prepared, moreover, for the employer to ask you for your insights into the field. The more knowledge of the basics you demonstrate, the more specific and helpful will be the advice you receive. Once you realize this, you'll understand why it is that if you go into the meeting simply asking about the very basics of the field (i.e., "I'm a big fan of Dan Rather's -- how should I get into the anchorman business, anyway?") you will demonstrate that you are a relative novice -- at best. If that's the impression you convey, the employer may be strongly tempted to give you the standard ten-minute spiel about the business, shake your hand, and get you out of the office as quickly as possible. Don't let this happen.

If you feel comfortable about the background work you've done up to this point, show the employer your research notebook. Mention an article or two you've read. If you've had any previous discussions with industry professionals, point these out, and discuss any new perspectives you've gained as a result. Be sure throughout all this that you are conducting a conversation with your contact, neither delivering a prepared monologue nor asking a staccato series of questions requiring immediate answers. You may find that your contact will give you the names of several people to get in touch with -- without your even asking!

Here's the secret that will allow you to maintain your panache throughout the Information Only Interview, and throughout the job search in general: virtually all employers are looking for good people. All the time. Period.

Good people are assets. If Ms. Tyman has no job to offer, it is only good business for her to recommend an outstanding candidate to someone else in the firm -- or perhaps even a friend elsewhere in the industry. She will, in the long run, benefit from this referral -- especially if you turn out to be a real star!

MENTORS

Mentors are very good people to have around in a job hunt. While this book is not the place to discuss all the ins and outs of the extremely complex subject of mentoring, it is certainly appropriate to address some of the issues you're likely to come across in the early levels of a professional job search.

What is a mentor?

A mentor is ...

interested in your career.

willing -- and eager -- to freely give you advice and help -- perhaps in your initial job search, but also as your career develops.

not necessarily your boss.

someone who likes you as a person, and also sees your potential as a professional in the field.

usually able to help guide you through potentially troublesome organizational and hierarchical areas that you might not navigate as successfully on your own.

someone who can provide you with access to important people and help make your successes more visible.

associated with your efforts on the job in other people's eyes.

usually a senior member of the staff or organization.

often a veteran with considerable experience in a given field.

While the seeds of a mentor relationship may very well be planted at this stage in your job search, it is virtually impossible to "establish" such a relationship in one meeting. Mentor relationships are sensitive to such factors as personal goals (both yours and your mentor's), the "corporate culture" of the firm, and personal chemistry. The advice at this stage is not to try to "catch" a mentor, but rather to be on the lookout for one. What you're really hoping to "catch" is the elusive setting that may eventually evolve into a mentor relationship.

One good signal in that regard would be locating a professional with whom you can openly and comfortably discuss your career strategy, and from whom you can accept constructive criticism. Of course, it helps to have someone who fills such a role in any endeavor, and the job search is certainly no exception. If a close friend or industry contact is helpful to you in mapping out your goals and methods, don't stop sharing things simply because he or she isn't a potential mentor!

ASKING QUESTIONS

As mentioned above, it's an excellent idea to be well-prepared for any kind of interview. That includes not only thorough research, but also having a good idea of the kinds of questions you'll ask.

Begin by asking your interviewer about his or her background. Most people, even if they're outwardly modest, enjoy relating their career histories. Your interest in how your interviewer spent those first few years in the industry is a sign of respect.

Many people will have fascinating stories to tell. Note any relevant anecdotes (once you've made sure that your interviewer doesn't mind your jotting a few things down during the course of your meeting). Such stories can be drawn upon and related at later stages of your job hunt.

Next, ask questions about the working environment.

What are the hours like? What are the people like? What sort of training or work background is usually required? What do people earn? (You may want to hold off on that last one until you're absolutely positive that the interviwer understands that you aren't looking for a job at this stage. It's a question that can be misread and can do unpleasant things to the "feel" of your conversation.)

If these questions seem to be producing a good rapport between the two of you, you'll probably want to continue along the same lines, entering into more specific areas. What does the interviewer like best (and least) about what he or she does during the day? What kind of skills are considered essential to his or her job? What are his or her career goals? Are there any landmark career choices your interviewer made years ago that might be decided differently now? Is there a cycle to hiring in the industry? What is the best strategy for approaching people? As a rule, should you start at the top when you contact someone, or should you begin at the department level? How long should a typical new employee expect to stay at one level? Is advancement best gained by staying with one company or by "hopping around"? Is there an advantage to starting at a small, growing firm, rather than a larger, better-known one?

In short, ask questions that can help you determine whether or not you're headed in the right direction. Ask questions that can identify what is important in the industry. Once you determine what's important, you can tailor your background to the needs of an interviewer in a discussion about an actual opening.

Above all, keep the conversation comfortable, relaxed, and easygoing. If you pay no attention to what your interviewer is saying (or isn't saying), and simply rattle away, checking off one question at a time, you are wasting the time of two very important people: the interviewer and yourself.

Make careful note of the answers you receive. If your interviewer wants to direct the conversation in another direction, don't resist. Keep an open eye for any signs that your interviewer is getting nervous about the next item on his or her schedule. Make every effort to be extremely considerate of your interviewer's time.

Once you've done all this, of course, you'll be ready to ask the big question, the one that will allow you to have a more promising job search at the end of the interview than you had at the beginning. Any guesses as to what that question might be?

Can you suggest anyone else that I might contact to talk about career opportunities in the industry?

ANSWERING QUESTIONS

Of course, you should be ready to answer some questions, as well. What should you expect to have to answer in the Information Only Interview? Probably some queries of a very general nature. Why are you interested in this industry? What were your college years -- or recent experiences -- like for you? What are your career goals? What are you good at?

But watch out. Just because the questions are general, don't assume that you can give general or vague answers in return. Most people make the mistake of appearing far too hesitant and undecided during a job interview -- and even though you can't ask for a job, you must treat the Information Only meeting as a job interview. The pressure may, in a way, be even greater than an actual job interview! Why? You've singled yourself out. You've done something very daring in asking for a meeting like this, something that only a tiny minority of job seekers will take the effort to do. No matter what the interviewer says, he or she is probably just a little bit impressed by your initiative. Now the question that's on the interviewer's mind is: Is this person for real?

The Information Only Interview will say more about you than it will say about the person you're speaking with -- no matter how much you jot down in your notebook. Make the best possible impression. Be every bit as decisive in person as you were in composing your letters.

Think carefully, ahead of time, about how you might approach the "basic" questions outlined above. Come up with some well-reasoned answers that point you logically in the direction of the industry you've chosen. If your background is in computers, and you've decided to go into banking, your career choice is going to need some explanation. Be prepared with an honest, easily understandable reason for your decision: perhaps you've developed substantial problem-solving skills working with computers, and are enthusiastic about applying those abilities to real-life situations that affect people directly. However you approach the matter, remember that you must do enough background work to know why you would be well-suited for the career area you're trying to enter. Stay away from responses that don't convey solid reasons for your decision. Answers like, "The banking industry is very exciting," while literally true, don't pass along any meaningful data to your interviewer, and do little or nothing to separate you from the pack.

Your career goals should be realistic. Your background should be stated in as positive and enthusiastic a manner as possible, and should support your stated professional desires. Wherever possible, try to link your strengths with those that you've determined are necessary for success in the industry -- and don't sell yourself short if you have specific positive accomplishments you can point to as evidence.

There's a reason for all this, and it's a simple one: the better the impression that you make with your interviewer, the more likely that person will be to help you out in your efforts to win a job.

The goal in any interview situation is to emerge with one of three things: a job, another interview, or a referral. Most people feel great after Information Only Interviews because the discussion is usually pleasant and the atmosphere encouraging. This can be misleading. If you haven't gained some tangible lead with which you can perpetuate your job hunt, the session has really been less than successful -- even though you may have gleaned some very important information. If, toward the end of your discussion, you haven't asked the "big question" I mentioned above, ask it. You may wish to follow it up with this one:

If I wanted to apply to your company for a position at some point in the future, with whom would I speak?

Always ask if you may use your interviewer's name when making contact, either with someone in the industry or with another department in the interviewer's company.

CONTACTS

This brings us to the question of contacts. The issue of the "contact network" has been outlined in broad terms a little earlier, but now that we've entered into the realm of the Information Only Interview, it's appropriate to go into a little greater detail.

The importance of contacts within an industry or company can never be overemphasized. Employers, as we know, will feel better about hiring someone that they know and like than they will about hiring a total stranger. That's why it's important that you not only utilize any contacts you may already have, but work actively to develop more. The simple fact is that the best jobs virtually always arise through word of mouth. You must have access to the "party line" employers use to fill these positions if you want to be considered for the most rewarding opportunities.

A good analogy might be the dilemma faced by someone looking for a parking place in a very crowded downtown area of a major city. Most people go around and around the block and up and down the side streets until they get lucky and find a spot. This approach is similar to the one you'll have to take if you embark on a job search with no contacts and no plans for developing any. It can take a long, long time to find anything.

On the other hand, imagine what finding a parking space would be like if you had a car-phone -- and six friends standing in strategically selected phone booths. The second that one of them saw a car pulling out of a spot, your number would be dialed, and you'd have up-to-date information on where you had to be, and when you had to be there, in order to get the spot. Now, if you could somehow set up such an arrangement, don't you think you'd find a parking place before the person driving around aimlessly waiting for "something to open up"?

That's the way it is in a job search, too. If you have contacts spread throughout the industry, you'll find out about openings much more quickly than your competition without contacts will. Don't be shy. Dive right in and ask for help. If your goals are realistic and your attitude that of a solid professional, you'll be surprised at how quickly you'll get positive results.

(As a practical matter, rest assured that it's far easier to establish a "career network" than it is to get your friends to stand in a cold phone booth for an hour and help you find a parking place.)

THE JOB INTERVIEW:
WHAT YOU'LL BE FACING

You've found out about a job at Fancy Footwork, the number three shoelace manufacturer in the country. Your contact at Ace Shoelace tipped you off when he got a call from a friend who works at F.F., as the firm's insiders refer to it. Your name has been mentioned to the right person, you made the call, and now you have an interview. Here's a real job opportunity at last.

In many ways a Job Interview is easier than an Information Only Interview: the focus is much clearer. There's a job description to look at, a number of requirements the position will entail, and a nice, solid yes-or-no answer waiting for you at the end. This kind of interview is much more predictable than the Information Only variety, because you know what the interviewer is thinking: Should I hire this person? And you already know the answer to that question!

There are a number of sub-groups within the broad

THE JOB SEARCH HANDBOOK

category of the Job Interview. You should be prepared for: a preliminary once-over; an in-depth interview which may be conducted by more than one person, but which will usually require that you meet with one interviewer at a time; a stressful "down-to-the-wire" session which may entail your confronting some intentionally difficult or even embarrassing questions; and a panel interview with more than one person interviewing you at a time.

THE ONCE-OVER INTERVIEW

The initial, or "screening", interview is typically conducted by an employee who is not in a position to decide whether or not to hire you. The whole point of this interview is to save the important people (i.e., the ones who eventually will make the decisions) the time it would take to gather a pool of talented candidates. So what's your interviewer's goal? Simple. To determine whether or not you're a "live one."

This is the point at which you must make your clearest, most straightforward presentation. The interviewer is looking for someone who fits the job description exactly. If, for some reason, you don't (and hardly anyone does), you'll have to make a strong enough impression to register with your interviewer as someone with valuable skills that compensate for some deviation from the "ideal".

It's especially important that you organize your own data before you enter this interview. Put more simply, you must know what you intend to say.

This may seem difficult if you've never interviewed at this level before, with this company before, or in this industry before. But the point is, broadly speaking, you can anticipate the types of questions you'll have to answer -- no matter where you're interviewing or how many times you've looked for a job before.

At this stage, you are going to be fielding questions that are open-ended and broad in nature. For example, many interviewers will ask you why you are interested in the position you've specified. Others will begin with a general question about your background. Still others could begin by inquiring about your current situation and why you are seeking a change (or, if you're a recent graduate, whether your skills are directly applicable to the position you're after).

Whatever the questions, you already know two things about them right off the bat. They are very likely questions that are to be directed not only at you, but at a number of other applicants at the same stage; and they will almost certainly be of such a general nature that you will have no difficulty preparing responses that stresses your strengths within the context of the question.

Suppose the position at Fancy Footwork you're after is one which requires two years of experience in a management-level position -- and you, Abigail Hunter, don't have it. Your strong sales background should help your chances, but the fact remains that you have your work cut out for you: show enthusiasm about the company, shine the spotlight on what relevant experience you do have, and convince the interviewer that you are worth, at the very least, another look, even though you don't meet the job description to the letter.

How do you do it? It's not really that difficult.

Because you show up fifteen minutes early, you have some time to take a look around the place. You notice that things seem a little disorganized, and that everyone looks a bit overworked. Your research on the company shows that Fancy Footwork is doing very well in some areas -- they have lots of orders. But they still need improvement in others: they're behind in shipping by two months and are constantly out of stock. You had a feeling that this company might need some management help; now you know they do.

You arrive at the door to Ms. Anna Shoestring's office -- she's the personnel administrator. You're asked to have a seat. While waiting, you notice some posters on the wall. The slogan: "We don't like any loose ends." It strikes you that it's an odd sentiment in such an (apparently) constant state of chaos!

You wait, trying to absorb every bit of information from

the environment. Fortunately, it isn't difficult: every four or five minutes a panicked employee rushes by clutching a late order from a customer, talking in hushed but tense tones about another critical shortage of some supply, or nervously checking a wristwatch.

Finally, fifteen minutes late, Ms. Shoestring comes out of her office to greet you. After shaking hands and exchanging hellos, you both walk into her office and take your respective places on either side of her desk. Though you know you've sent her a copy of your resume, she's misplaced it. You offer her a duplicate you happen to have brought along for just such an eventuality.

"Ms. Hunter," she says, "you've probably noticed we're pretty busy around here. Let's get down to business. What interests you about our sales manager position?"

At this point most prospective employees would pause, gulp, and try to come up with something that doesn't sound like a stammering dodge of an answer, but, alas, is one nevertheless. It all seems so abrupt! She didn't even ask about that high-school debating trophy!

However, you are ready! You know what's really going on. The interviewer is, in essence, actually asking you something like this: "Can you please save me some time, show some initiative, and show me that you're fantastic?" Sure you can -- when you think about it, there's really an unlimited number of ways for you to do exactly what your interviewer wants!

Given what you've learned about the company, it's probably best to address what you can identify as the big problem the company faces: the chronically busy environment and impossible schedules.

You begin by pointing out that a sales manager position is a logical next step for you, given your strong sales background. Then you support this by relating some of your experiences: the time, for instance, that you brought in so much business to your family's firm that the orders backed up production by three weeks. You go on to outline how you solved that problem by setting up a customer service hotline, and by working with the production people your father hired over the summer so you could understand their problems a little better.

In other words, you speak in specific terms about how you've solved problems in the past -- and can be expected to do so in the future. What's more, the problems you solved are associated closely with the ones the company itself is going through right now. What's the result of giving an answer like that?

Wham! You're a "live one." You've distinguished yourself from the fifteen other people Ms. Shoestring has spoken to that day, and you've done it in about forty-five seconds, which saves her a heck of a lot of time, and probably engenders a certain amount of goodwill between the two of you immediately. The beleaguered Ms. Shoestring has found exactly what she was looking for all along. She doesn't care now whether or not you have two years of professional management experience. She's got a feeling you can get the job done. By being open to the employer's problems and how your background could allow you to solve them, you've been able to tailor your answer in the correct way.

Look at what's happened closely. You had a prepared answer about your past experiences that demonstrates your problem-solving abilities, preferably in a way that parallels the employer's own problems within the company. Whatever question the interviewer decided to use as the interview's "opener" -- you were prepared to shape your answer around a strong statement of your strengths. You used specific examples that showed off strong past performance and future potential. And you maintained an enthusiasm tempered with professionalism -- in the hopes of revitalizing a glazed, overscheduled, easily bored, or just plain overworked interviewer.

The "telling stories" strategy is a very useful one. Use it for the rest of the interview whenever possible. Make sure you've prepared many examples of your skills that can be used as miniature case studies. These incidents will bring to life any statement you make about your own strengths. It is much easier for an interviewer to recall your skills and background if you've related some memorable anecdote that illustrates key achievements.

Think back to the teachers that you liked best in school. Didn't they usually pepper their lectures with a lot of examples -- examples that somehow brought the subject to life for you? Do the same thing with your own experiences.

Even in the "screening" interview, some questions may come up that don't seem to lend themselves to anecdotal or "story" answers. Many of these questions are asked in order to determine your current employment status, your ability to think on your feet, or your long-term potential: Why are you thinking of switching jobs? What do you know about our company? What would make you uncomfortable about this position? What would you consider to be your chief weakness?

To the extent possible, outline answers to these kinds of questions ahead of time. Whatever your state of preparedness, answer the question in a positive context. For example, if you are leaving your present job because you're afraid that the company is going to close, don't say you're worried about job security and want to get while the getting is good. Be positive. Stress the attributes of the company with which you're seeking a position, and talk about how you want to work within a company that is in a growth cycle or has a reputation as the leader in its industry.

Never be negative. Whether it's discussing a former employer, evaluating your past supervisors, or even responding to a request that you list the things about yourself that should be considered weaknesses: don't yield to the temptation to malign a former associate or advertise the fact that you type poorly. Find a way to respond in a way that illustrates some strength.

How? Well, suppose Ms. Shoestring is a very tough interviewer and throws that very question at you -- the one where you're supposed to talk about your weaknesses.

Ms. Shoestring: Ms. Hunter, could you outline for me what problems someone like you would have in handling this position?

Admittedly, this is a toughie. But if you make your "problems" a group of qualities that are actually slightly

90

overenthusiastic positive attributes, you'll be well on your way to answering the question in a way that puts your candidacy in the best possible light.

You: Well, I've had to accept the fact that you can't always push others as hard as you might push yourself. I remember one instance where I probably alienated someone I was supervising at my current job by asking him to produce more than he thought was possible, and it led to a little friction between us. Of course, we were able to resolve that problem successfully -- I invited him to lunch the next day, and tried to get his perspective. We get along great now.

An answer like that shows that you are a creative manager of people, that you're oriented toward high standards when it comes to productivity, and that you know how to respond to a nasty question! That last element means more than you might think -- who do you think is going to be tougher to deal with, a personnel administrator throwing a trick question, or a customer who ordered something from Fancy Footwork six months ago and hasn't received it yet?

The key, again, is to try to show your "weakness" in action -- in a way that silently advertises your strengths.

That mindset should stay with you throughout your interview. Try to project the image of a person who can solve problems and get the job done. Think of that image in a positive way from the very first second you walk into the building. Think this is an exaggeration? Many studies indicate that an interviewer makes an initial decision about an applicant within the first three minutes of an interview. After three minutes, you're either building on a positive impression or attempting to recover from a poor one. It is crucial to project a positive, "problem-solver" image from the very beginning of your meeting with the interviewer.

It should come as no surprise that you would be well advised to prepare an outline of everything you hope to cover in your interview. Don't go overboard by trying to "script" the whole appointment, but do take care of the basics

Make sure that you've matched your skills and background with the requirements for the job, and that you can speak intelligently about both. As in the Information Only Interview, be prepared with some questions -- but be ready to cut the questioning short at the slightest hint that your interviewer's schedule is too full to accommodate them. Try to stay with questions that focus on the company you're applying to and the specific details of the job. Stay away from premature or potentially sensitive subjects such as salary, benefits, or the long-term financial position of the firm.

Finally, know exactly what's on your resume. Don't laugh. A surprisingly large number of candidates have been eliminated because of an inability to intelligently discuss their background as documented.

The point of all this planning is to make sure that you feel strong about your performance once the interview is over. Your aim is to feel as confident as possible that you will be judged by what you feel to be your best attributes.

And be sure not to forget the overall goal of any applicant undergoing a "screening" interview: get a second interview!

PASSING THE FINAL EXAM:
THE SECOND INTERVIEW AND BEYOND

You've made such a fantastic impression on Anna Shoestring that she wants you to talk with the managers of the other divisions -- and perhaps even with Mr. Footwork himself, the president! Now what?

In the second and subsequent interviews, your goal changes. And not a minute too soon. By this point in the job search there's a very good chance that you're flat-out sick of referrals, advice, screenings, and other indirect and crooked byways. Now (finally) you're after the job!

It's important at this point to determine who your potential boss will be -- before you go any further into the interview cycle. That person becomes very important to you now, not only because you may well be working for him or her in the near future, but, more importantly, because your potential supervisor is almost certainly the individual responsible for making a final hiring decision.

Sometimes your prospective boss will be easy to spot -- especially if you're applying to a small organization. In a large company, however, there are often many layers of managers. This makes your job more difficult.

The best way to get this information is often to ask for it. When you're arranging your next interview, inquire (tactfully!) what position your next interviewer holds -- and who your supervisor would be if you were selected for the position.

Armed with the name of the real McCoy, you can proceed in your interview cycle with confidence, as you'll know who should be the target of your responses. You'll also be on the road to finding out what the supervisor feels is required from a successful applicant, which can be a very different thing from what a personnel administrator considers important.

Frequently, you'll be seeing several people. As I've already mentioned, many companies will organize a search committee to provide the boss with as many viewpoints on a candidate as possible. Always keep in mind, however, that there is almost always one person who makes the final decision, and that person is the individual you want to receive your most polished presentation.

Interviewing is a skill you can develop -- a skill akin to taking an exam. You can anticipate the kinds of questions you will receive in a test. So you study your material, run through it until you're confident that you know it thoroughly, then prepare various responses prior to actually taking the test. When the time finally comes to take the test, you're eager to see how well you've anticipated the contents of the exam. The better you've prepared yourself, the more fluent, coherent, and lucid you'll sound to the professor when your work is reviewed.

The same principles hold true in the advanced interviews. The better prepared you are, the more confident you'll be when you step into the office and field questions. That confidence will be one of your most important assets in the interview. Because you're confident, the content of your answers will be superior. The rough edges that were once in your presentation are gone. You will have cut out the unimportant parts of your "pitch" and highlighted those that are critical. For the second and subsequent interviews, you must do more than convince someone that you're worth another look. You must convince your future employer that you're the only one worth considering.

In short, you must go into overdrive.

By this point, you've probably already read as much as you can about the industry. You've interviewed contacts within the field. You've created the perfect cover letter and resume. And you've had at least one interview with the company that went very well. What else can you do?

Admittedly, you've accomplished a great deal, and most people would consider themselves ready for the second interview at this point without too much more preparation. However, there are a few more pieces of information available to you, and they might just give you that extra boost as you approach what baseball fans call the "stretch drive."

Certainly, more information about Fancy Footwork would be in helpful. If F.F. is a large corporation, there's a decent likelihood that it's publicly held. If it is, you should be able to get detailed information from a special business report called a "10-K." This report goes into even more detail than the annual report you may have seen earlier. The "10-K" also tends to be more objective in its appraisals of the company; it's the official report the company must submit to the Securities Exchange Commission each year.

You may find this report in a large public library, or perhaps in the library of a local public university. Review it carefully, even though there may be a great deal of accounting and government jargon that can be difficult to penetrate. Get whatever you can from the report, paying special attention to any comments on the company's growth and goals.

If the company is small or privately held, you won't find any public reports. In this case, the best way to get more information is to ask the company itself. (It's probably not a bad idea to do this for the larger companies as well.)

Virtually every company has some kind of promotional literature, brochures, or fact sheets that you can review. Now that you've made it to the second round of interviews, it won't seem unusual to request such information.

Other strategies include doing an article search for newspaper or trade publication pieces about the company. Most such periodicals have some sort of index you can use to look for references to your target company. In addition, any good-sized library will be able to provide you with access to general periodical indexes, through which you can investigate any number of headings. Though this process can take some work, you may discover a *Business Week* article describing the fifty most promising mid-sized apparel firms, and mentioning Fancy Footwork prominently. This type of data is invaluable -- it offers a third-party assessment of the company's status. You can use whatever facts you come across in this "overdrive" research effort in your next meeting with your interviewer. Such an effort will undoubtedly leave an impression that you're both thorough and remarkably enthusiastic.

You might also go back to any contacts you've had up to this point who may know something about the company in question or its employees. These contacts can give you important insights into the perceived problems and strengths of the company. Most of your contacts will be eager to help at this point once they see that you've made real progress. Nothing makes contacts feel better than actually helping someone -- because you may in turn be in a position to help them somewhere along the line!

HOW THE QUESTIONS WILL CHANGE

Prepare for slightly different and more difficult questions in your second interview. Remember that tough questions are in fact a very good sign: you've passed the initial test, and now merit close examination.

In specific terms, you should be ready to address questions that begin with, "What would you do if...?" Such queries are designed to get an idea of how you would handle common situations or problems you are likely to encounter on the job.

These questions are difficult to prepare for, because, realistically, there are an infinite number of scenarios with which you may be presented. However, there are some techniques that may prove effective for the hypothetical interview question.

The best bet is to use your past experience as a guide. In other words, parallel the situation you're given with something you have already encountered, and explain how you successfully solved that problem. Indicate that you would probably use a similar strategy on your new job. Admittedly, this will require a certain amount of thinking on your feet -- and, to some degree, that's what these questions are designed to measure -- but hypotheticals can be confronted successfully if you keep your poise, make as many connections to your background as possible, and remember to prioritize the problems you are presented with. (An employer may throw a "curve" in this type of question by outlining three problems, one or more of which is of significantly lesser importance than the rest. Which will you address first?)

If you draw a blank when it comes to past experiences, you should use the best common-sense answer you can think of and conclude by pointing out that you'd probably consult with your co-workers for advice and guidance. This way, even if you give the "wrong" answer (and occasionally there will be *no* "right" one) your interviewer will respect logical powers, and be impressed by your willingness to ask for help.

There is one final dilemma you may encounter in an interview: the unanswerable question.

Interviewer: Well, Ms. Hunter, that's very impressive. I just have one more quick question for you before we finish here. It's obvious you've had a lot of exposure to the shoelace field: please tell me what the highest-rated domestically-manufactured shoelace is with regard to stress tolerance.

Don't even *think* about guessing. Even if you somehow get lucky and guess correctly, a smart interviewer will sense your nervousness and may well "subtract points" for bluffing.   Here's your best answer if you simply have no idea what the correct response is to a technical stumper like the one above:

You: Well, I don't know the answer to that one, but I'll guarantee you that I can find out!

As long as you don't use this technique with too many questions, you can count on making the best impression by simply telling the truth -- you don't know.

THE EXTENDED INTERVIEW

In general, it is important to be well rested for your second round of interviews -- but it's particularly crucial if you're scheduled to spend a great deal of time with a potential employer.   You may be asked to spend the entire day at the company, with the firm picking up your lunch and dinner tab.   (Who said there's no free lunch?)   Some employers will, if you've travelled some distance for your interview, even put you up for the night somewhere!

Catnaps on the plane notwithstanding, you'll probably find in these cases that it's very difficult to be at your best for eight hours straight or more.   Your face will no doubt feel like plastic after a morning of nonstop smiling, and your voice will eventually crack after a couple of hours of respectful, soothing, attentively enthusiastic tones.

Take any opportunity to "freshen up": this may mean a visit to the rest room, or could entail a brisk walk around the block alone.   During those few private moments, try to relax and shake out some of your nervousness.

Mealtimes   present   interesting   situations   for   the interviewee. New kinds of questions and anxieties surface: What do I order? Should I ask for an alcoholic drink? Should I relax a bit and open up -- be more human? Should I talk about business only or move on to outside interests? What if the menu is printed in Albanian?

Leaving aside the matter of foreign-language menus, let's look at the problem of what you should order. It is very difficult to resist the temptation to order a fancy meal at the expense of the interviewer's company. Nevertheless, resist. Though you may be eager to consider your meal roughly comparable to being taken "out on the town" by a rich relative, this is not what's taking place.

The most prudent way to handle lunch interviews is to follow your interviewer's lead -- or, if that's impractical for some reason, simply order something that you'd normally select if you were the one paying the bill. Keep your selection within reason, and try not to order pizza and a Diet Coke if your interviewer's selected beefsteak tartar. Whatever you order, keep it light. You want to be free to speak and express yourself intelligently throughout the lunch. Imagine trying to do that while attacking a plate of unshelled oysters with a side of corn on the cob.

As far as alcohol is concerned, use your best judgment. Take your lead from your hosts. If they are having Perrier and lime, then you know the answer to the alcohol question. On the other hand, if your interviewer casually orders a double boilermaker, and then looks your way with an expectant smile, it may be wise to partake in some reasonable way so as not to offend your host.

One important note: if you know that one beer sends you off Niagara Falls for the next 48 hours, you should definitely avoid any alcohol whatsoever. Whatever you do, don't lose points that you've gained in your interview. Be sure to keep an eye open for any obvious institutional biases on the part of the interviewing firm. Different approaches will be in vogue at the House of Seagram than you'll encounter at the Mormon Tabernacle Choir.

Topics of conversation during an "interview meal" usually wander from those that are strictly business. But beware: no matter what the mood of the meal, you are being evaluated. Avoid politics. Try not to bring up controversial issues. Don't engage in heated ideological or philosophical debates -- even though you should be sure not to appear to give in to every opinion of your interviewer. In short, try to enjoy yourself without initiating undue friction.

WHAT TO WEAR

While the issue of apparel is important throughout the interview process, it becomes, for many people, a major issue once they reach the advanced interview. In a way, your second or subsequent interview should bring you closer to the mark in terms of knowing what to wear -- because you will have already seen the signs of the company's unwritten (or written!) "dress code" in your first interview.

Don't go overboard on your wardrobe, no matter how much you may read about "power" clothing. Your objective when it comes to dress is to fit in -- not to overwhelm. No one should have to go out and buy a new top-dollar suit for the sole purpose of interviewing. On the other hand, if you don't have any kind of suit, you'd better go out and buy one (unless, of course, your professional goal is to become a lifeguard).

The most useful advice about dressing for an interview should come from the people you see in the company. Make a mental note of what they wear. A two-piece or three-piece suit? Wingtip shoes? Pumps or high heels? Dark or light shades?

If you get confusing or contradictory signals, you might ask your industry contacts about this issue, or even check photographs appearing in the company literature at your disposal.

THE DECISION-MAKER

All of the guidelines for advanced interviewing can be condensed into one sentence: Convince your next boss that you're worth hiring.

If you make an excellent impression on the person who'll finally make the hiring decision, you will, obviously, have a strong chance of landing the job.   Once this person decides to hire you, any others in on the hiring process will have to produce strong arguments against your appointment. Many search committee members, by the way, are reluctant to insist that *any* candidate be hired.   Sure, Abigail Hunter's presentation is very strong, but what if things don't work out? What if there are problems with the training?   What if this person botches some huge project?   *Then w*hat will the boss think of the guy who recommended adding Hunter to the payroll?

Welcome to the wonderful world of corporate decision making.

The interaction you have with your prospective boss, then, is all-important.   Even if your interview with this individual is at the end of the day, make every effort to be as energetic, enthusiastic, and professional in bearing and appearance as you possibly can.

Remember that your arsenal of accomplishments and achievements may not have reached the decision-maker directly.   If at all appropriate, restate your positive attributes and relate some of the anecdotes that convey your problem-solving capacities.   Do not assume that these pieces of information have been passed along from your earlier interviews.

ONCE YOU'VE REACHED THIS POINT...

Guess what?   Though you may repeat the process a number of times before you find the perfect "fit," at this point, there's every reason to expect that you'll be offered a position.   You not only know your industry and target companies inside and out, you've also written outstanding job search letters, composed perfect resumes, negotiated the intricate mazes of direct calls to employers, breezed through initial interviews, and proven yourself a potential "star" in front of the person who may be your next boss.

So what else is there to life?   Once they offer you a job, isn't that all she wrote?   Isn't this the end of the job search process?   And why are there still all these pages left before we get to the end of the book?

In one sense, a professional job offer is the end -- of one phase of your job search. But in another sense, it's just the beginning.

CHAPTER FOUR:
Negotiations, Careers, and Job Satisfaction

MANAGING YOUR SUCCESS

Congratulations! You won the job offer.

Though it may seem irrelevant, there remains one very important question for you.

What on earth do you do now?

Many people at this stage might simply say "yes" to the first real opportunity and be done with the whole business of hunting for a job. However, you should bear in mind that upon receiving that offer, you are, for once, in a position to negotiate.

It is at this point, for instance, that you can begin asking pertinent questions about salary, benefits, and promotions. You should make sure that you understand all of your boss's expectations, and that your boss is aware of what you feel you are truly worth as an employee. In short, it's time for each side to make clear its intentions. That's how good working relationships start.

Obviously, you're going to have to avoid hitting your prospective employer with a rapid-fire series of "60 Minutes"-style questions. Nevertheless, there are a number of important issues which you must begin to investigate before you can consider accepting the position you've been offered.

Be sure that you know, at least in broad terms, the answers to questions like these: What is the firm's review and evaluation process? What are the benefits being offered? Is an advanced degree necessary for advancement to top positions? What is the last person who held this position doing currently? Who is the formal supervisor? Is this person different than the actual supervisor? What are the firm's hours of operation? When is the busy season? Does the firm have any immediate expansion plans?

EVALUATING OFFERS

Sometimes people work so hard to get a job offer that they miss the fact that they don't really want the job. Strange but true.

Suppose, for instance, that you, Abigail Hunter, have been developing leads in the shoelace industry in order to find a job in management. You have, as we may recall, excellent sales experience, but limited shoelace exposure. In developing your leads, you've made many contacts, and along the way, you've met Roger Retread, the sales manager at Amazing Lace, the third largest shoelace manufacturer in the country. He likes your credentials, your meeting goes very well, and you feel confident he may steer you toward the management position you're after, either at Amazing Lace or elsewhere within the industry. Then Mr. Retread surprises you.

He offers you his top sales job in the most lucrative territory in the country.

Suppose you were to throw your earlier desire to move into management out the window. Then what was the point of all your work conducting the job search? But suppose you tell Roger the job's not for you. Are you sure you won't lose any sleep over taking a pass on that kind of opportunity?

It's a tricky situation, not least because there's very few things more disruptive to your psyche than accepting a job that you hadn't planned on. Why? Because there's no better way to get someone to offer you the job that you do want, and can't take without shooting your resume full of holes.

Make no mistake. All job offers deserve careful evaluation. Even the most unlikely position can hold potential you might not immediately acknowledge. But the point is, you have to choose to take advantage of that opportunity.

So. What are the best techniques for evaluating offers? One approach is to resort to the time-tested "pros and cons" list.   Take a sheet of paper and draw a vertical line down the middle.   On the left, write "PRO;" on the right, "CON."   Now ask yourself some questions.   For instance, what are the positive aspects of the job?   Which elements would challenge you or give you the greatest pleasure?   Write these points down on the left hand side.   Then ask yourself what parts of the job would deviate from your "ideal."   Are there any potential personality problems with any coworkers you've met so for?   Is the location less than perfect?   Write down any of these items on the right hand side of the sheet.

If a great many negative points arise from this process, be careful not to make a hasty acceptance.   Ask yourself some questions: Does this job really meet my needs?   Do I have a good opportunity for advancement?   How is this job different from my present situation?

You may even want to go back to your contacts, mentors, or other advisors and ask for some objective opinions.   Often, you will learn about some exciting (or nightmarish) new aspects of the position you may have overlooked.

Your contacts might also be able to give you salary estimates and ranges that will help you determine whether or not you should accept the salary you've been offered or prepare a counteroffer.

Finally, take a moment to evaluate your future boss.

If at all possible, take the time to talk to the last person who held the position you've been offered.   He or she will have the freshest insight into the dynamics of the working relationship you'll inherit.   As you listen to any accounts of former (or current) employees, keep in mind that their points of view, by definition, will not be objective.   You'll have to closely evaluate the person making the comments, as well as your potential boss.

If you don't have the opportunity to talk with the person whose shoes you may fill, you'll have to rely on your own instincts.   If you feel unsure about the personality, integrity, and/or sincerity of the person you'll be working for, think twice about accepting the job.

Why should you be so careful on this point?   Ask anyone who's ever quit or been fired from a post because of personality problems with a supervisor. You can be working for the number one company in the industry, in the greatest city, for a fantastic salary -- and still be miserable if your boss is a jerk.

Ideally, you want a boss who cares for you as a person, and who would like to see you advance and prosper. While this may not be possible in every case, you should still be on the lookout for the kind of relationship that allows your good performance to benefit your boss nearly as much as it does you. If, however, your boss is threatened by potential and intelligence in general -- and yours in particular -- you're going to have problems. And, in all likelihood, you're going to have no one to turn to for help.

Case in point: consider the situation of a recent college grad who interviewed with one of the top advertising agencies in New York. He was overjoyed by the offer he received and accepted immediately. It turned out that his boss (whom he had never met) was the company slave driver. She ate assistant account executives for breakfast, demanding regular overtime, offering almost no training, and providing little or no exposure to higher-ups when a job was (somehow) well-performed. Our hero began to think (without real justification) that advertising might not be for him after all -- simply because he'd latched on to a member of the Genghis Khan Fan Club.

Take a good look at the futility of his situation. Meeting the "standards" his supervisor regularly held him to was clearly impossible. He knew that complaining would do little good, and could actually harm his future prospects by setting him apart as a troublemaker. The boss's personality was definitely not the kind that lent itself to a "heart-to-heart" conversation over coffee; she simply considered her subordinates dirt and treated them accordingly. (Such managers are, sadly, not as rare as one might wish.)

Finally, the poor fellow decided to quit -- which didn't do wonders for his resume. And what exactly was he supposed to say when asked in a subsequent interview about exactly why he left his previous position?

So remember: your new job is only as good as your new boss.

NEGOTIATION

Suppose you've decided that you are close to saying "yes" to your prospective employer, but are disappointed with the salary (or the job title, or the benefits, or the bonus plan -- whatever). What to do? Negotiate!

Don't worry about losing your job offer. Think about why you got it in the first place. The employer believes that you're the best person available. A great deal of time and effort has gone into your selection, and the last thing the employer wants to do is reopen the search.

Believe it or not, you've got some negotiating power. Use it, but don't let that power spoil a perfectly good opportunity, either. If some aspect of the position is less than you had hoped, discuss it reasonably with your employer. Come right out and say (politely) that you had hoped for a higher salary, larger bonus, or better health plan. Ask how flexible the company can be in arranging your entry to the firm. And be sure to have a specific goal in mind for any element of the package you attempt to negotiate. In most cases, the employer will ask what would make you happy. This usually leads to some kind of compromise.

What's the worst thing that could happen? The employer could refuse, and say something like, "I'm sorry, but the starting salary is set by company policy and is non-negotiable." At least you know where you stand and have a decent glimpse into the corporate "mindset" on these matters. More likely, the employer will tell you that he or she can't give you a final answer immediately, and will contact you within a specific time-frame with an answer to your request.

In either case, you should decide ahead of time what your action will be if your request is denied, or if you're offered less than your goal. Usually, the employer will try to make you happy -- because the happier you are, the harder you'll work and the better your results will be.

SOME DILEMMAS IN
"WINDING IT ALL UP"

Most job hunters who are actively pursuing a career-oriented position will have several choices in front of them at this stage of the game. As a result, there's a good chance that the first offer you receive will not be your first-choice position. Even if you've been able to come to this conclusion using the methods outlined above -- what do you say to the "second-choice" employer?

This is, frankly, a difficult situation. Basically, you have two choices: accept the job and terminate discussion with other prospects, or say "thanks, but no thanks" to your "second-tier" contact and hope for the best.

Many job seekers would offer a third alternative: accept the "second-tier" job, keep your other applications active, and write a letter of resignation if something promising comes up two weeks later.

Wrong.

Playing "footsie" with anyone in an industry you've spent this much time trying to get into is, quite simply, nuts. Even if you were somehow able to keep word of such a back-door maneuver from reaching other employers in the short term (which is doubtful), you will have thoroughly and intentionally burned a bridge, which is the ultimate sin in any contact network. You never know how deeply you may eventually regret the decision to mislead a potential employer.

There is a technique you can use to ensure that the greatest number of possibilities remain open. It's an effective little method called "stalling."

Ask the employer offering you a position how much time you have to make your decision. Be honest and say that you have many active possibilities that you must terminate amicably. Be prepared for some tight scheduling: unless you're entering some kind of special training program, chances are that you'll have no more than one or two weeks to decide what to do. This is enough time, however, to contact all your leads and relate your story.

What story?

Tell all other potential employers that you have an offer, and that because you're still very interested in their company, you'd like to know where they stand on your candidacy. This tactic will often encourage quick action, and result in the firm supplying you with a definite yes-or-no answer before your deadline.

Now, after trying this, it's great to hear something like, "You're in, Abigail; we feel you're going to take the shoelace field by storm, and we don't want our competitors at Amazing Lace to have the first crack at you." But what if the response you get is a little less clear-cut?

If you feel you're getting mixed signals, or are unclear about what you should do after talking to the company in question, try to look at the "subtext" beneath the message you receive. A few examples of some "hidden messages" you may be given are featured below.

"That's great to hear, Abigail; I don't have an answer for you right now, but my feeling is that it would probably be a good idea for you to seriously consider taking the offer from Amazing Lace."
("You're not my first choice for the position you applied for here, but you may be in the running.")

"Can you delay your final decision for a couple of days and let me get back to you, Abigail?"
("You're a strong candidate, but I need to talk it over with someone else and/or take another look at how you stack up against the competition.")

"Amazing Lace, eh? (Pause.) Do me a favor. Give me until tomorrow afternoon and I'll try to see whether I can push this through Personnel -- the job's supposed to be posted for a full month internally, but I don't think there's really much competition for the job inside the company."
("I want you to work for us. There are some bureaucratic hurdles I still have to get over. Don't tell Amazing Lace anything until I talk to you again.")

At some point, you will have to make your final decision. If you decide to reject an offer, fine. You're the kind of candidate who can expect to receive multiple offers and can pick and choose. If you decide to accept, congratulations! You've just begun a new chapter in your ever-evolving work life.

ENDING THE JOB HUNT IN STYLE

You have the job you want, a good boss, and a competitive salary and benefits package. You're done, right? Not so fast. You should still be sure to build on all the good work you've done so far.

One job does not a stellar career make. There will be other searches down the road, and when you begin them, you're not going to want to start from scratch. It would be a real shame to waste all those good contacts you made over the course of your job hunt, wouldn't it? Now is the time to solidify those contacts.

Write to each of the contacts who helped you in a significant way. Everyone who gave you important advice or a useful lead should hear about your good news. All these people are going to remember you -- not only because they helped you get a job, but also because you thanked them in writing. (You'd be surprised at how rare a thank-you note is in the job-hunting world.)

If you become a real success in your field, your next job opportunity may not come as a result of your efforts. You may be contacted by a search firm on the lookout for talented people, or one of your contacts may eventually try to steal you away from your present job. This is all very flattering (which never hurts), and may also lead you to examine some interesting career possibilities. Keeping your contacts up-to-date on your progress is one very good way to encourage such interest in your career.

PLANNING YOUR
FUTURE AND CAREER

Many people look upon their "career" as the job they presently occupy. Unfortunately, this is a very short-sighted perception of the way careers usually develop. Gone are the days when most people stay with one company for forty years. In fact, the executives in many companies depend on turnover for new faces, fresh ideas, and rekindled enthusiasm. It makes good sense to look at each job you hold as one step along a career path that will help you to build a fruitful and fulfilling work life. If you have a plan -- or at least a broad philosophy of career development -- you'll find that a career need not be confined to one narrow field or industry.

For example, suppose you're a teacher dedicated to influencing and educating as many children as possible. After ten years of teaching, you might decide that a change would be refreshing. You're now interested in exploring other ways of influencing children. You decide that textbook publishing is another route to the same end (having a positive effect on children). So you conduct a successful job search in the field and become a textbook editor for a small publishing firm.

Most people would define this sort of move, from teaching to editing, as a career switch. It really isn't. It's a continuation of the initial goal.

Suppose that after five or six years of editing textbooks, you decide that you'd like to write them. You become a freelance textbook author -- in effect, a consultant to publishing firms. Again, it really isn't a career switch at all.

After a couple of successful years in this area, you decide that you could do a better job actually publishing the textbooks yourself. So, at the age of 41, you begin your own publishing firm. But you're still pursuing your original goal -- reaching and educating children.

Of course, this sort of industry-hopping may not appeal to everyone. It's not unusual, though, for people to hold four or five jobs within the course of one career -- jobs that can have substantially different descriptions, objectives, and working environments -- and remain true to a "fundamental" career goal.

Most people remain in the workforce for more than forty years. That's a long time to stay in one job or industry. Even if you do decide that one industry gives you the best long-term career, you should constantly set professional goals for yourself, and constantly monitor them.

Suppose you've been with the same firm for twenty years. You're perfectly happy in the shoelace industry, but you find that there is no room for advancement at your present company, New England Lace and Eyelet. Your search may not stray very far from your present region, and you may decide that it makes sense to target New Jersey Consolidated Shoelace as your top employment prospect.

You may feel reluctant to move on after building such a strong history (especially if doing so means missing out on a substantial retirement package). But it won't hurt you to look. In fact, you may find that the positive reception you find waiting for you at New Jersey Consolidated will not only serve as a big confidence-booster, but also provide you with the leverage to negotiate a better deal with your old friends at New England Lace and Eyelet.

Throughout your career, ask yourself the important questions about your continuing efforts in the workplace: Are you happy? Are you still learning? Do you feel accomplished? Are you developing skills? Are you correcting your weaknesses? Are you receiving regular raises and promotions? Are you making more and more friends within your industry?

CHANGING YOUR CAREER GOALS

If you can regularly answer "yes" to most of the questions just posed, you probably shouldn't worry too much about analyzing your career path.

However, most people's career priorities do change over time. Goals are either achieved left unrealized. New opportunities arise. Interests change. If you come into the job search process determined to earn a lot of money, and then win a job which pays you more than you ever thought you'd earn, for a while it's going to be a lot of fun. But there's going to come a time when you have to set another goal for yourself. (For some people, that goal is, "Earn more money than anyone else in the country." It's an interesting goal, with interesting ramifications.)

Eventually, you're going to have to ask yourself, "What's next?" And the way you answer that question will, in large measure, determine what you'll do with your career. The evolution of a career is usually cyclical in nature. Your expertise, skills, talents, and interests will develop over the course of time, and at some point, you'll probably feel that you've explored the field to the limits of your interest. You may decide to begin another exploration process in another field. Some people have the interest and dedication to make one job or field last their entire career. This is the exception, rather than the rule. Most people -- and careers -- are ever-changing propositions. Sometimes the changes will be ones that you'll initiate; sometimes they'll be beyond your control.

Once you accept the idea that change is an integral element of your career (and, in a broader view, your life), it's much easier to view what might once have been considered "upheavals" in a positive, even enthusiastic, way.

Make no mistake. Career changing can be tough. If you've been in banking for your first fifteen years in the "real world," and at age 36 suddenly feel the urge to explore a career as a professional opera singer, you've got a lot of work ahead of you. On the other hand, if you decide to leave banking to help manage an opera company, you may have a comparatively easier time achieving your goal.

As mentioned in Chapter One, changing careers takes time and careful planning. Examine your objectives closely, and think twice before leaving your current job. Bear in mind that, unless you are fresh out of college or grad school, any employer will view you somewhat suspiciously if you're unemployed. You'll have to fight off all sorts of stereotypes about jobless people, and you'll make the employer ask a number of tough questions that you may or may not be given the opportunity to answer directly: Did this person get fired? If not, why did he or she quit? Were there problems with attendance, morale, or insubordination? How long can this applicant be expected to stay with our company?

Remember: unemployed people make employers nervous.

If at all possible, keep your present job and spend your non-work hours exploring new careers. In the beginning stages of a job search, a great deal of work can be done in off hours, especially if you make your lunch hours, personal days, and vacation time count for as much as possible.

The goal of career exploration at later stages of your work life changes subtly. You want not only to find a new, exciting position for yourself, perhaps in an entirely new area, but also to see how your old experiences might relate to the new ones. Identifying transferable skills is always important when looking for a new position.

Most employers will ask themselves, "Why should I even consider hiring this person who has no specific experience in my company's industry?" You must answer this question directly even if it is never put to you in words. Address the issue head-on when you first make contacts within the new industry. There is no way you can hide your work background. Take the offensive. Admit the lack of specific industry experience, then emphasize the wealth of related experience you have.

Determining your related experience, of course, can be hard work, but it is absolutely necessary if you hope to successfully transfer your skills from one industry to another. Unless you're willing to begin at the very bottom of the career ladder, you must convince a prospective employer that you are not only a good candidate, but also worth considering for a position well above entry level. This will take work, but can be accomplished.

DEALING WITH SETBACKS

Somehow, somewhere, at some point in your job search, something will probably go wrong. Whether you're trying to find your first professional position or attempting to transfer skills you've built up over decades, there will inevitably be problems.

Your attitude or philosophy toward your career is extremely important. If you're approaching a change in your work life from a negative point of view, that feeling will pervade any interview situation you might encounter -- even if you have been recently fired, do justifiably hate your present job, or are legitimately bored with your existing career path. In some instances, you may be better advised to postpone your search for a new career until you can approach the search itself from an optimistic and enthusiastic point of view. If this means finding temporary work while you recover from a disappointing situation, so be it. Don't handicap yourself with the emotional burdens of a bad situation.

Keeping morale high during your job search is important. Get help from friends and mentors. Anyone who has helped you with career questions or other matters will probably offer support and worthwhile suggestions for making a change.

It is important to keep in mind that any career change is possible, given the proper dedication and talent. In other words, if you have a great voice, perseverance, and enthusiasm, you *can* make the change from professional banker to opera singer! (Both Ulysses S. Grant and Harry Truman rose from lackluster careers in business to successful ones in national politics. Elvis Presley began his career as a truckdriver. Major league pitcher Jim Lonborg, who won the Cy Young award in 1967 while leading the Boston Red Sox to the American League pennant, is now a successful Massachusetts physician.)

THE TEAM PLAYER —
AND THE "WE" GENERATION

Many people spend a great deal of time analyzing themselves and their careers, trying to define their "perfect job." It's a healthy thing to do, but don't get carried away. Too much analysis leads to paralysis. It's entirely possible that your "perfect job" may be beyond your reach, or, worse, beyond anyone's reach. Don't be crushed if you end up "compromising," because, to a large degree, compromise is the name of the game.

If you bring a self-centered approach to your job search, it will be very difficult to reach your goal. If, on the other hand, you approach the job hunt with the goal of trying to analyze the goals of your future employer as well as your own, you'll realize that there are many roles that you can fill quite competently -- and achieve a high level of career satisfaction.

Don't be concerned that this point of view will lead to your being exploited. When working for a concerned employer, you'll find that he or she will take great pains to reward you for your good work. Remember that it's much easier for an employer to keep a fairly steady staff than it is to be in a constant hiring mode. Even in the largest corporations, where hierarchical political concerns can make or break careers, analyzing the employer's point of view can make the crucial difference.

If you look upon job hunting as the process of making friends, you'll have come very close to the central idea of this book. What the method boils down to is a team approach: one that allows you to reach your own goals as well as those of the team. Team players, interestingly enough, tend to know a great deal about what's occurring in their workplace. That's a big advantage. If you know what is going on around you, you'll be better prepared for what might happen -- as well as what you can *make* happen.

Often the best friends are those who have many things in

common, but leave room in their relationship for significant differences. These differences become the cementing agent to the friendship because they keep the relationship fresh, productive and satisfying. By providing your employer with the attitude, intelligence, and skills he or she needs, you can actually go further than *getting* a job: you can *create* one in which your special talents can provide you with a happy and satisfying career.

It's all a part of working together to form the best possible product line, the best possible business, the best possible company, and the best possible work life. Not only for yourself, but for virtually everyone you come in contact with. That's the key, and if you bear it in mind as you execute your job search (and on the job, where you'll be challenged to put your talents to their fullest practical use), you won't be able to *avoid* career satisfaction.

Much of the advice on careers you'll find outside of this book will advocate a fashionable degree of narcissism in planning and executing your job search. Many experts will ask you to adopt a "me-first" attitude in posing and answering the questions that accompany any career: What do I want? How much money can I get? How fast can I move ahead? Which employer is offering me the most?

Such attitudes are, in today's workplace, open to increasing suspicion on the part of many employers and senior executives -- and rightly so. Interestingly enough, the "me generation" mindset not only clouds one's ability to formulate and achieve group goals (which is, in a very real sense, what working in a company is all about), it also seems to provide less long-term personal growth and career satisfaction. The irony, of course, is that those employees who put aside all the "me-first" nonsense are frequently the ones who arrive earliest at the very career destinations so attractive to the success-at-any-cost-crowd. So much for the "me generation."

Welcome to the "*we* generation!"

APPENDIX:
Assessing Your Skills, Identifying Goals, and Doing the Research

PRE-SEARCH RESEARCHING

This section of the book is for those job seekers who feel they need to sharpen their research skills before they attempt to pursue the next step in their career -- or who want some help in defining a clear career goal in the first place. Of course, if you completed these steps some time ago, but have been out of the job market for a while, you may want to review this section just to be sure you've touched all the bases before beginning your search.

In a way, defining your career goal is considerably more important than "hitting the books." It's a bad idea to do a lot of research into the shoelace field if you're not certain that that's the industry for you. No matter what your friends, family, or teachers may tell you about how much of a "natural" you are for a given profession or work area, be sure to examine any career field carefully before you commit to it.

KNOW WHAT YOU WANT

It's a fact of job search life: before the resume, before the cover letter, before the first phone call, before *anything,* you must decide what you want to do next with your career -- or, if you've just gotten out of school, what you want to do, period.

If you don't know what's next -- and especially if you're unhappy with your current position -- it may be tempting to say to yourself, "I don't *know* what I want to do; I just know I don't want to do *this* anymore. I've got a feeling that whatever my next job is, I'd rather do that than this!"

Such a reaction is a perfectly acceptable response, as long as you can move on from there. The "I-gotta-get-outta-here" mentality can provide you with sufficient motivation to solve the next problem: what do I do next?

Many books have been written on the subject of

identifying the right career goal. And most of the advice contained within them boils down to two basic questions:

What do I enjoy?

What do I do best?

Answering that first question might seem fairly simple. A lot of people would answer (somewhat flippantly), "Okay, here's what I enjoy: playing golf, watching *All My Children*, and drinking beer. Now what's my new title: Vice President for Leisure Oversight and Calorie Consumption?"

It's true. If you want to identify realistic options, it may be more appropriate to find another way to phrase Question Number One, though it remains a valid test of your overall career direction. How about something like this:

What do I enjoy most about my present job (or work-related experience)?

Come up with some positive answers: I like talking with people; I enjoy solving problems; I get a kick out of working for a big, prestigious company; I like to write; I enjoy research; I love coming up with ways to save time and money; I feel good about the kind of work my company or oganization is doing.

If you can't think of anything positive, start writing down how much you love golf and what your favorite episode of *All My Children* is, and work from there. Keep writing. Keep thinking. Come up with as many things as possible that you'd like to do -- or think you'd like to do.

What you're doing is compiling a list of tasks, job characteristics, and even general ideas that you enjoy. Try to make it as long as possible by carefully considering virtually every aspect of your work life so far, even summer jobs and high school and college employment. The longer your list, the greater your possibilities.

Be honest with yourself. Don't put items on your list that are fanciful or vague. Remember that you'll have to ask yourself Question Number Two before too long.

ASSESS YOURSELF

What do you do best?   Most people begin their answer to this question by reciting the practical skills they've developed over time.   This is a good way to begin, if only because it gets you started with facts you know intimately. So scribble away.

Perhaps you: type 70 words per minute; compose excellent leters; have an eye for fashion; draw accurate maps; always keep everything perfectly organized; know how to balance the books; take stunning photos; repair things around the house almost by instinct; know how to throw a successful party; work well with computers.

Write it all down.   You'll probably discover that some of the answers to your second question have elements in common with the answers to the first one.   That's a good sign.

Each of the skills you identify become direct or indirect indicators of general areas of aptitude (in layman's terms, they tell you a lot about what you can do for a living).

Be sure to include skills you may have developed in "non-work" environments.   Most people don't realize that their free-time activities often reveal a great deal more about themselves than what they do during "office hours."   Don't ignore skills you've developed simply because they're not work-related.   They *are* work-related.

Suppose you're an excellent cook.   Your friends and family always accept your dinner invitations eagerly. Silence descends over the table when your meals are served, because everyone's too busy to talk.   Leftovers never seem to materialize after your feasts.

You are, actually, an *amazing* cook.   So what?   Well, there are almost always some important work-related skills that are part of performing any task well, and cooking is certainly no exception.   Even though it may sometimes be difficult to convince employers of the direct applicability of these skills, it's important that *you* know that they exist, and know how they can shape what you decide on as a career.

Think about it.   A good cook must be able to follow directions carefully, practice careful time-management, and organize things effectively.   Most cooks have to develop interpretive skills to make sense of confusing or inconsistent recipies from time to time.   And, finally, cooks must be adept problem-solvers.   When things go wrong and the souffle falls twenty minutes before the guests arrive, an ability to operate efficiently in a "crisis atmosphere" doesn't hurt.

These aren't bush-league skills.   If you can honestly say to yourself that you've developed them over the course of time as a cook, you've got a pretty good "package" with which to start.   Then your task would be to highlight and/or further develop those skills in such a way that a potential employer can see them just as clearly as you do.

For this process to work, however, you must be just as honest with yourself as you were in answering Question Number One.   Once you make an evaluation, talk it over with your friends to see if they agree with your assessment. You might ask them to name the skills *they* think you have and compare notes.

Try not to overestimate your skills, but don't slight yourself, either.   Take on the whole problem with an even-handed approach.

It's not easy to come up with these lists.   But doing so is an important step you shouldn't overlook, because the lists are excellent tools you can use to determine your next step. If you feel you aren't getting the kinds of ideas that make sense, it may be a good idea to find a career counselor, psychologist, or other objective third party whose professional opinion you respect.

FINDING THE
"PERFECT" JOB

After engaging in the soul-searching exercise outlined above, you should have some pretty good lists in front of you.   Now it's time to see how these lists match with the job descriptions out there in the "real world" -- and determine which professional avenues you'd like to explore.

How many times have you heard someone begin a complaint about their job with the words, *"If only I didn't have to worry about money, I'd..."*? Well, let's try to put that question to practical use. If you didn't have to worry about money, what *would* you be?

Go ahead: take a stab at answering it. Your answer will give you a starting point, and you'll be able to move on in your search for the "right" position all the more easily.

Career exploration is like prospecting. You start digging expecting to find one thing, and you often end up finding something else. That "something else" may well be more attractive to you than your original goal! Skeptical? Here's an example.

Suppose you answer the question about your "dream job" like this:

I'd like to be an investment banker and make approximately $1,000,000.00 per year.

Fine. If you are a student, teacher, machinist, homemaker, or holder of any of a thousand other positions, you might consider the prospect of becoming a millionaire somewhat remote. But go ahead anyway. Start a research project. Your goal is to find out what big-time investment bankers do and how they get started. With some persistence, a telephone, and a couple of trips to a local library, you can begin making real progress.

By reading about the field, you'll get an idea of the professional requirements and attributes of succesful investment bankers. If you can show a little initiative, make some phone calls, and talk to some people in the field, you'll get a better idea of what goes on behind closed doors, and you'll get a sense of what kind of people investment bankers really are. You'll also get a sense of how you might fit into the world of high finance.

Can (or should) everyone become an investment banker, then? No. One guarantee, though: it isn't as difficult to approach your goal as you might think, if you take the necessary steps. What's more, your goal may change significantly once you do take those steps! In this case, you'd probably learn a great deal about other fields related to investment banking: commercial banking, stockbrokering, insurance, accounting, computers, commodity markets -- in short, a wide variety of professions *you may never even have heard of before.*

These fields are exciting, not only because they're in the same general field as your "dream job," but also because they could turn out to be even more attractive -- once you ask some fundamental questions about the people who *work* in the "dream" every day.

For instance, what kind of hours are usually expected from investment bankers? What is a successful financier's "typical" background? What kind of values do people in the industry have? Are there any sacrifices that must be made in terms of time with one's family, self-worth, personal growth, or even average lifespan? Maybe money *isn't* everything -- what do investment bankers get out of their jobs *besides* a big paycheck?

The more information you find, the closer you'll get to the *real* "dream job," and the easier it will be to join the ranks of the company you eventually choose. Research the fields that interest you the most right now, and let yourself be adventurous in deciding where it goes from there. If another career sounds interesting, follow the lead and take some time to examine it. Look closely not only at the obvious aspects of the job -- work descriptions, environment, money -- but also the "intangibles" such as peer relationships, effects on personal values, and the potential for long-term career satisfaction.

Consider openly the many consequences that will accompany any decision to pursue a career goal. If you are thinking of changing career fields after a long time in one industry, for instance, what sort of sacrifices will you have to make to retrain yourself in a new profession? Do you want to make those sacrifices? *Can* you make those sacrifices?

Go beyond the obvious when searching for a career. Don't risk long-term unhappiness and the morale-destroying cycle of finding yourself in a continual career-replacement mode.   Enter careers consciously, with an eye toward what really makes you happy.   If you give yourself enough time for the process, you'll eventually come up with some very exciting prospects.

THE PAPER CHASE:
WHERE TO GET INFORMATION

Preparation and research are basic steps in any job search, and the library is the best place to begin your preparatory and research work.

Not surprisingly, many reference librarians are excellent career counselors.   After all, they're experts at tracking down information.   They are familiar with the needs of people initiating a job search.   They can give you an idea of the age of the sources you'll be working with.

Armed with your list of interests and talents, try to isolate four or five industries that seem to address your strongest points.   Then talk to the reference librarian, and tell him or her that you're exploring careers and would like to get as much information on your target fields as you can. (For a list of the books that can help you most, see the Bibliography.)

Bear in mind, though, that there is only so much you can learn about careers through books.   Although many are quite detailed (the U.S. Department of Labor's *Occupational Outlook Handbook*, for example) any field you read about can change significantly within a period of a few months or even weeks.   A quick survey of the copyright dates of the books on virtually any reference library's shelves will convince you that you'll need some up-to-date resources, as well.

The "non-book" sources you'll want to explore include industry journals, newsletters, and periodicals -- often called trade magazines.   Once you've settled on the industries you want to know more about, these are the publications that you'll probably want to spend the most time examining.

Almost every industry has one or more periodicals that virtually no one outside the business reads.   While it's often difficult for an outsider to understand much at first reading, try to take the time to decipher as much as you can. Keep track of phrases that are unfamiliar, as well as prominently mentioned companies and individuals. Before too long, things will begin to make a little sense. Not a lot, mind you, but enough to give you some idea of what's going on in a given field.

Another good reason to read the trade publications is that many of them feature extensive job listings. An employer is much more likely to address the "select" readership of a trade magazine than to broadcast an opening in the Sunday papers.

You may also find material of interest in the annual financial reports of individual companies in a certain field. All public companies must register with the Securities Excange Commission, and are required to furnish certain business information to their stockholders and the general public on a regular basis. These reports can be found in the business reference sections of most major libraries, usually in the microfiche files.

Annual reports outline the financial progress (or decline) of a company over a given twelve-month period. The first part of the report usually discusses in broad terms the firm's operations, products and services, and facilities. The second section gives an overview of the company's financial position, often either explaining away poor performance with a summary of extenuating circumstances, or concentrating on the more profitable areas of the business while downplaying less successful ventures. Of course, if a company is doing very well, this section will all but glow with the satisfied, self-congratulatory prose of corporate success.

Finally, the report focuses on numerical charts and graphs that support the rest of the report's conclusions. Unless you've got an accounting background, this section may not make a lot of sense to you at first. There's usually some accompanying text that will give you some idea of what's being communicated. Get as much as you can out of this section, but don't panic if things don't click automatically. If you'd like to know more about this subject, you may want to consult John Tracey's excellent book, *How To Read A*

Financial Report.
You'll get some idea of the firm's "corporate culture" by the general look of the annual report. Is the layout flashy or conservative? What did the company decide to emphasize on the cover? How are the people in the photos dressed? (As mentioned earlier, such clues can help you determine what *you* should wear to the interview.)

THE PSYCHOLOGY OF THE
WANT AD – AND THE PERSONNEL OFFICE

Another source of information about careers is the classified section of your local newspaper. Many people consult the newspapers first, and consider them a primary source for generating employment leads. This is not a good idea (for reasons explained below), but it is suggested that you go through the want ads on a regular basis -- to glean information you can use in your job search.

Ask yourself what the ads can tell you about the industry you've selected, or about a particularly interesting position you may come across. You'll find you can discover quite a lot this way. Prepare questions you can attempt to answer through the ads you review. Is there an industry that tends to advertise more than most? In the field you've selected, which do you come across more: entry-level, middle-management, or executive positions? Do the companies you're following usually give their name and address, or do they merely list an anonymous box number? What work experiences seem to be the most important for people looking for the type of job you want?

Why can't you just buy a Sunday paper and use it to generate leads? Well, there's no law that says you can't try, but there's a real problem you'll run into almost immediately: everyone else does exactly the same thing. And you don't want to be like everyone else. You want to stand out.

What would motivate an employer to pay for a classified ad in the first place?

Think about it for a moment. Would you put an ad in the paper if you didn't have to? What happens when you put an ad in the Sunday paper? You're faced with a blizzard of resumes and phone calls. You have to take scores of messages and evaluate dozens of resumes. You interview lots of possible candidates, most of whom will be rejected outright.

If you were a manager trying to fill a key position without upsetting a calendar full of pressing projects, you'd probably avoid want ads like the plague. And this is exactly what most employers do. The vast majority of companies would rather find a candidate through professional referrals, ads in trade magazines read by those already "in the industry," or college placement offices. From the employer's perspective, pleading for a qualified applicant in front of 100,000 or more avid job seekers means spending time away from their real focus of business.

Nevertheless, you can get a great deal of information from reading want ads. Use them intelligently, and remind yourself that you're probably not getting a perfect picture of the "true" job market. When you see an ad in the paper, it usually means one of two things: either the company is listing the position because of an obligation to fulfill equal opportunity employment regulations; or the employer is trying desperately to find the right person, no matter what it takes.

It is remarkable how many ads appear every day in daily and Sunday newspapers, given all the trouble companies usually have with them. Such "traffic" considerations are one reason why so many large businesses organize personnel offices to handle the time-consuming job of publicizing openings and finding new people.

Pity the poor personnel administrator. His or her office is asked to find the perfect candidate for the job, and goes about doing so by reserving ad space when necessary, publishing job descriptions, collecting and screening resumes, and rejecting most candidates through initial interviews. Of course, in the case of professional positions, the personnel office itself is rarely responsible for hiring anyone, but concentrates instead on identifying unqualified applicants before sending on the "hot prospects" for further examination. Ninety percent of the time, it's boring. Ten percent of the time, you find someone interesting, but someone else gets to do most of the interviewing.

Whether or not you try responding to a want ad (and a great many companies will channel you through the personnel department whenever you apply, publicized opening or no), remember that the person you're talking to is a professional resume-rejecter. Before you do anything else, be sure that you have found a convincing way to answer the unspoken question, "Why should I recommend you to the department head?"

Sample Job Search Notebook Worksheet

Company Name: _Ace Shoelace Company_

Contact: _Tyrone Layssus_ Title: _Marketing Manager_

Source of Contact: _Phone Research_

Address: _14 Wingtip Place_
Shoetown USA
_12345_

Phone: _(999) 555-9876_
extension: _11_
best times to call: _8:00 AM - 9:20 AM_

Letter Diary:
First letter sent: _11-30-88_ Type: _CHALLENGE_ Follow-up: _Call_
Second letter sent: _____ Type: _____ Follow-up: _____
Third letter sent: _____ Type: _____ Follow-up: _____

Calling Diary:
First call made: _11-28-88_ Outcome: _Got information, name, title_
Second call made: _12-4-88_ Outcome: _Arranged informational interview_
Third call made: _____ Outcome: _____
Subsequent calls: _____ Outcome: _____

Interview Diary:
First Meeting: _12-8-88_ Who: _Layssus_ Outcome: _Suggested I speak w/ Tie R. Less._
Second Meeting: _____ Who: _____ Outcome: _____
Subsequent Meetings: _____

Company Information: (size, strengths, products, etc.)
One of the top shoelace manufacturers in the country.
Velcro closure expansion due soon.

Trade Magazine: (frequency, article references, subscription cost)
Fit To BE Tied, monthly; June article "Ace: No Longer on A Shoestring"
_$125_

Comments & Rating: (what do you think about this company?)
Industry leader with excellent promotion policies.

BIBLIOGRAPHY

BIBLIOGRAPHY

The directory publications listed below should be available at most large metropolitan or university libraries. Each is useful for gathering information about various career paths. Once you explore careers using these publications, you'll have a solid foundation on which to build the rest of your job search. *The Harvard Guide to Careers* is recommended especially highly, primarily because its career bibliography is perhaps the most comprehensive available.

Other publications can be found in most retail bookstores.

Chapter One

The American Almanac of Jobs and Salaries. John W. Wright. Avon, New York, N.Y., 1984.

Dictionary of Occupational Titles. 4th edition, U.S. Department of Labor, U.S. Employment Service, U.S. Government Printing Office, Washington, D.C., 1977.

The Directory of Directories. James M. Ethridge, editor. Gale Research Company, Detroit, Mich. Biennial.

Encyclopedia of Associations. Katherine Gruber, editor. Gale Research Company, Detroit, Mich. Annual.

Guide for Occupational Exploration. U.S. Government Printing Office, Washington, D.C. 1979.

Harvard Guide to Careers. Martha P. Leape and Susan M. Vacca. Harvard University Press, Cambridge, Mass. 1987.

How to Read a Financial Report. John A. Tracey. Wiley & Sons, New York, N.Y. 1980.

Hudson's Newsletter Yearbook Directory, 6th edition. Margaret Leonard, editor. Hudson's Newsletter Directory, Rhinebeck, N.Y. 1986.

The IMS Directory of Publications. IMS Press, Fort Washington, Penn. Annual.

International Publications Directory, Vol. 5 of *The Working Press of the Nation.* The National Research Bureau, Inc., Chicago, Ill. Annual.

The Job Bank Series. Bob Adams, John Noble, Michael Fiedler, Brandon Toropov, and Carter Smith, editors. Bob Adams, Inc., Boston, Mass. Various local titles; various publication dates.

The National Job Bank. Carter Smith, editor. Bob Adams, Inc., Boston, Mass. Annual.

National Trade and Professional Associations of the United States. Columbia Books, Inc., Washington, D.C. Annual.

Occupational Outlook Handbook. U.S. Department of Labor, Bureau of Labor Statistics, U.S. Government Printing Office, Washington, D.C., 1979. Annual.

Occupational Outlook Quarterly. U.S. Department of Labor, Bureau of Labor Statistics, Washington, D.C. Quarterly.

Standard Periodical Directory. Oxbridge Communications, New York, NY. Biennial.

Chapter Two

Executive Jobs Unlimited. Carl R. Boll. MacMillan, New York, N.Y. 1987.

Chapter Three

The Resume Handbook. David V. Hizer and Arthur D. Rosenberg. Bob Adams, Inc., Boston, Mass. 1986

Resumes That Work. Tom Cowan. New American Library, New York, N.Y. 1983.

Chapter Four

Knock 'em Dead with Great Answers to Tough Interview Questions. Martin John Yate. Bob Adams, Inc., Boston, Mass. 1985

Sweaty Palms: The Neglected Art of Being Interviewed. H. Anthony Medley. Ten Speed Press, Berkeley, Calif. 1984

Appendix

Harvard Guide to Careers. (See above.)

Job Search Strategy for College Grads. Susan Bernard and Gretchen Thompson. Bob Adams, Inc., Boston, Mass. 1984.

What Color Is Your Parachute? Richard N. Bolles. Ten Speed Press, Berkeley, Calif. Annual.

INDEX

INDEX